# PETER and ANTHONY SHAFFER

## a reference guide

*A*
*Reference*
*Guide*
*to*
*Literature*

Jackson Bryer
*Editor*

# PETER and ANTHONY SHAFFER
## a reference guide

### DENNIS A. KLEIN

## G.K.HALL &CO.

70 LINCOLN STREET, BOSTON, MASS.

**Library of Congress Cataloging in Publication Data**

Klein, Dennis A.
  Peter and Anthony Shaffer, a reference guide.

  Includes indexes.
  1.  English drama—20th century—Bibliography.
2.  Shaffer, Peter, 1926-      —Bibliography.  3.  Shaffer,
A.  (Anthony),  1926-       —Bibliography.  I.  Title.
Z2014.D7K55     [PR736]     016.822'914      82-2962
ISBN 0-8161-8574-3                               AACR2

*This publication is printed on permanent/durable acid-free paper*
MANUFACTURED IN THE UNITED STATES OF AMERICA

For Jill, Gerie, and Ira Brian

in loving memory of my mother

# Contents

# The Author

Dennis A. Klein received his Bachelor's and Master's
degrees from the University of Kansas and the Doctor of
Philosophy degree with a specialization in modern Spanish
drama from the University of Massachusetts. Although
most of Dr. Klein's major publications have been on the
Spanish playwright Federico García Lorca, he also wrote
2 volumes on Peter Shaffer for the Twayne English
Authors Series. He is a regular contributor to the
García Lorca Review and Hispania and was a contributing
editor for García Lorca:  A Selectively Annotated Bibliography of Criticism. Dr. Klein is a member of the
committee which compiles the International Bibliography
for the Modern Language Association. The author is
presently a Spanish professor at The University of
South Dakota.

# Introduction

Peter and Anthony Shaffer are unique in that they are twins, both of whom have distinguished themselves as playwrights. Peter Shaffer has been a prominent figure in the British theater since his first play, Five Finger Exercise, opened in London in 1958. Since then, his plays have won international acclaim in his native England, in the United States, and throughout the world. With the production of Equus in 1973, Shaffer won a permanent place in the history of British and world drama.

Criticism on Peter Shaffer, once the domain of drama reviewers, has spread to the literary and even the psychiatric communities. This phenomenon is not surprising given the breadth and depth of his plays, which include outrageous farce, domestic drama, historical spectacle, philosophical inquiry, and psychological penetration. Few critics are indifferent to Shaffer's plays; they are either lavish in their praise or outspoken in their condemnation. The Royal Hunt of the Sun has inspired the greatest division among critics, some labeling it a showy fraud and others lauding it as a profound, theatrical event. Amadeus, Shaffer's most recent play, has provoked a similar reaction. Of his other plays, the critics are in general agreement that Five Finger Exercise is a meticulous study of family life, that The Private Ear and The Public Eye are witty and sophis- ticated, and that Black Comedy is hilarious farce. The over- whelming popular and critical success of Equus speaks for itself, yet an occasional critic demonstrates dissatisfaction with the "bargain basement" psychology and fails to recognize that it was Shaffer's purpose to tell a story within the theatrical idiom, not to mention to present a thought-provoking theme.

Anthony Shaffer's career has been a more diverse one than his brother's. Before becoming a playwright, he practiced law and worked in television advertising. Although his first play, "The Savage Parade," was performed in 1963, it was so completely forgotten that when critics were raving about Sleuth, they hailed it as Anthony's

ix

first play. (Their oversight was apparently never corrected, and five years later they were calling <u>Murderer</u> his second play.) Much of Anthony Shaffer's writing talents have been devoted to film scripts, including such notable works as "Frenzy" and "Death on the Nile." Unfortunately, criticism on film scripts does not fall within the scope of this bibliography, since "Frenzy" was more closely identified with its director, Alfred Hitchcock, and "Death on the Nile" was more closely identified with Agatha Christie who wrote the original novel, than they were with Shaffer. He also wrote the film script for brother Peter's "Black Comedy." Perhaps in part since Anthony's dramatic oeuvre is considerably less prolific than Peter's, perhaps because only <u>Sleuth</u> had real success on the stage, he has not inspired the critical attention in journals that his brother has.

All bibliographies are selective, and this one is no exception. The primary concern is with reviews of and articles on the plays of the Shaffer brothers (although there are some biographical items and reviews of their early novels). There are limits even within this narrow realm; it would have been impossible, not to mention impractical, to include all reviews, since their plays have been presented in every corner of the world. Therefore, I have included only the reviews of the major productions in London and New York. In the cases of <u>The Royal Hunt of the Sun</u> and <u>Black Comedy</u>, which had their debuts at the Chichester Festival, reviews of those productions are, of course, included.

I have listed only those editions of the plays which contain commentary on the texts. Not every book of the "Who's Who" variety is mentioned, if it carries no more than a brief sketch available in fuller form elsewhere. Likewise, newspaper articles that mention only ticket prices, changes of casts or a specific actor's or actress's performance are generally omitted. I have not included reviews from local neighborhood newspapers. (I did not consider the <u>Village Voice</u> a local neighborhood newspaper.) Of the many books on modern British drama, only those that treat the Shaffer brothers are found here; many of the others that omit Peter Shaffer are listed in my bibliography in <u>Peter Shaffer</u> (Boston: Twayne, 1979). I have attempted to include no "blind" entries. With very few exceptions, I have seen every item listed in this bibliography. The few items in foreign periodicals that I was not able to verify, I have indicated with an asterisk and have given the source of those references. Many of the newspaper and broadcast reviews that I read are from the Billy Rose Collection at the Library for the Performing Arts at Lincoln Center. Some of the items did not have page numbers. I have located as many of the items as possible in the newspapers from which they were extracted; unfortunately, some of the newspapers are no longer in existence, and others are not available in this country. In those few instances where I have left an entry without a page number, the review is available at Lincoln Center.

# Introduction

In my commentary on newspaper and magazine reviews, I have
attempted to balance the amount of space devoted to interpretive
comments with that devoted to evaluative comments on the plays. I
have also balanced, to some extent, direct quotations from the reviews with my paraphrasing of them. Where a word or short phrase is
involved (i.e., _excellent_, _a hit_), I did not use quotation marks, as
I did to signify that I have quoted at length the words of another
writer. In an effort to avoid confusion, I have written separate
sections for Peter and for Anthony Shaffer. Articles that apply to
both of the Shaffers, I have listed under Peter and given a cross-
reference to Anthony. The cut-off date of December 1980, allows me
to include the reviews of Peter Shaffer's _Amadeus_ and Anthony
Shaffer's "The Case of the Oily Levantine."

I thank the reference and interlibrary loan departments of the
I. D. Weeks Library of The University of South Dakota for their
valuable assistance, as I do the research and theater collections of
the New York Public Library, both on Fifth Avenue and at Lincoln
Center. Special thanks go to Mr. Monty Arnold at the Billy Rose
Theatre Collection whose expertise saved me many hours--or perhaps
many months--of research time. I thank Professor Jeffrey Berman, of
the Department of English at the State University of New York at
Albany; J. Alexis Burland, M.D., of Bala-Cynwyd, Pennsylvania;
Sanford R. Gifford, M.D., of Boston, Massachusetts; James W. Hamilton,
M.D., of Milwaukee, Wisconsin; Jacob E. Slutzky, Ph.D., of Roslyn
Heights, New York; and especially Jules Glenn, M.D., of Great Neck,
New York, all of whom helped me through their correspondence and
with copies of their articles. Thanks also go to Dr. Robert Stoddart,
formerly of the Department of Classics of The University of South
Dakota, for his expert translation of the article by Dieter Schultz.
Likewise, I thank Professors Donald Pryce and Gerald De Jong of the
Department of History of The University of South Dakota for trans-
lating the titles of the articles in Polish and Dutch, respectively.
Finally, I thank the Student Financial Aid Office of The University
of South Dakota for providing me with the efficient secretarial
assistance of Miss Debra Limoges and the clerical assistance of
Mr. Ricardo Colón.

# PART I
# PETER SHAFFER

# Chronology

1951    The Woman in the Wardrobe (novel) published in Great Britain under the pseudonym of Peter Antony.

1952    How Doth the Little Crocodile? (novel; with Anthony Shaffer) published in Great Britain under the pseudonym of Peter Antony.

1955    Withered Murder (novel; with Anthony Shaffer) published in Great Britain.

1956    Withered Murder (novel; with Anthony Shaffer) published in the United States.

1957    How Doth the Little Crocodile? (novel; with Anthony Shaffer) published in the United States.

1958    Five Finger Exercise opened at the Comedy Theatre in London on July 16.

1959    Five Finger Exercise opened at the Music Box in New York on December 2.

1962    The Private Ear and The Public Eye opened at the Globe Theatre in London on May 10.

1963    The Private Ear and The Public Eye opened at the Morosco Theatre in New York on October 9.

        "The Merry Roosters' Panto" opened at Wyndham's Theatre in London on December 17.

1964    The Royal Hunt of the Sun opened at the Chichester Festival on July 6; at the Old Vic by the National Theatre Company in London on December 8.

*Chronology*

1965    Black Comedy opened at the Chichester Festival by the National Theatre Company on July 27.

The Royal Hunt of the Sun opened on October 26 at the ANTA Theatre in New York.

1967    Black Comedy and White Lies opened at the Ethel Barrymore Theatre in New York on February 12.

1968    Black Comedy and The White Liars opened at the Lyric Theatre in London on February 21.

1970    "The Battle of Shrivings" opened at the Lyric Theatre in London on February 5.

1973    Equus opened at the Old Vic by the National Theatre Company in London on July 26.

1974    Equus opened at the Plymouth Theatre in New York on October 24.

Publication of Shrivings (New York:  Atheneum).

1979    Amadeus opened at the Olivier Theatre by the National Theatre Company in London on November 2.

1980    Amadeus opened at the Broadhurst Theatre in New York on December 17.

# Writings about Peter Shaffer

## 1956

1  BOUCHER, ANTHONY. Review of Withered Murder. New York Times,
   11 March, pp. 26-27.
        An attempt at a detective story in the Grand Manner.
   Writing is often literarily amusing.  The trick solution
   is both banal and preposterous.

## 1957

1  BOUCHER, ANTHONY.  Review of How Doth the Little Crocodile?.
   New York Times, 3 March, p. 31.
        Markedly better than last year's Withered Murder.  In-
   genious virtuosity of plot artiface.

## 1958

1  ANON.  "Children vs. Parents:  Subtle Play at the Comedy."
   Times (London), 17 July, p. 4.
        Five Finger Exercise has the greatest claim to dis-
   tinction of all the recent plays exposing parents to the
   bitter reproaches of their children.  The father is too
   stupid to be believable and is a weakness in the play.  The
   son struggles to safeguard his inner-self in the midst of
   his parents' quarrels.  The dialogue is of a rippling
   subtlety.

2  ANON.  Review of Five Finger Exercise.  Times (London), 20
   July, p. 9.
        "Mr. Shaffer may easily become a master of the theatre."

3  ANON.  "Sir John Gielgud to Produce a First Play."  Times
   (London), 10 June, p. 5.
        Announces opening of Five Finger Exercise at the Arts
   Theatre in Cambridge on 30 June 1958, before being pre-
   sented on the West End.

1958

4  BRIEN, ALAN. Review of <u>Five Finger Exercise</u>. <u>Spectator</u> (25 July):133–34.
      The family is real. Shaffer takes no sides: there are no heroes and no villains. Dialogue has pace and bite, but no great wit. Shaffer is a keen observer.

5  DALLAS, IAN. "The Naturalists." <u>Encore</u> (10 September):24–28.
      On the crop of new Naturalist playwrights, of which Shaffer was one. Shaffer is a born dramatist because he is first and foremost an architect. Exact and revealing psychology. The fault of <u>Five Finger Exercise</u> is its too-strict adherence to the Naturalist pattern. Soul-searching tirades. The future of the British theatre lies in part with Shaffer.

6  DARLINGTON, W. A. "New Author Heartens West End Reviewers." <u>New York Times</u>, 17 August, sec. 2, p. 1.
      <u>Five Finger Exercise</u> portrays creation of the relationships and tensions that arise as a result of the arrival of the tutor. Each characterization rings true. Shaffer has mastery of theatrical technique.

7  GIBBS, PATRICK. Review of <u>Five Finger Exercise</u>. <u>Daily Telegraph</u> (London), 17 July, p. 10.
      Views the tutor as the source of disruption of the mother–son relationship by unwittingly attracting both mother and son.

8  HOPE-WALLACE, PHILIP. Review of <u>Five Finger Exercise</u>. <u>Manchester Guardian</u>, 17 July, p. 5.
      Mrs. Harrington compensates for an unhappy marriage by becoming an intellectual snob; Walter worships his adopted family. Shaffer lacks the ability to create sympathy for the pathetic characters.

9  KEOWN, ERIC. Review of <u>Five Finger Exercise</u>. <u>Punch</u> (23 July):118–19.
      Overpraised but crammed with promise. Shaffer has something to say and says it skillfully.

10  M., A. "Compelling Sincerity of <u>Five Finger Exercise</u>." <u>Stage and Television Today</u> (London), 24 July, p. 9.
      The best play on the West End in a long time. The inconclusive ending suggests that it will all start over again after the curtain falls.

11  MARRIOTT, R. B. "Peter Shaffer Calls for Magic and Mystery." <u>Stage and Television Today</u> (London), 31 July, p. 8.

1958

> Shaffer is opposed to playwriting that does no more than satisfy the fantasies of the writers and perhaps a few people in the audience. A play must be a work of art and shaped like a Chinese vase or a sonata.

12  POPE, W. MACQUEEN. "A Promising New Dramatist Who's Not Angry Young Man." New York Morning Telegraph, 29 July, [page number not available].
> Splendid character drawing and natural dialogue, spiced with wit and knowledge of life in Five Finger Exercise.

13  RICH. Review of Five Finger Exercise. Variety, 23 July, p. 58.
> Shaffer writes intelligently, with keen insight into his characters; but there are confusing moments, and one cannot always tell if Shaffer is trying to write a psychological drama or a slick comedy.

14  SHULMAN, MILTON. Review of Five Finger Exercise. Evening Standard (London), 17 July, p. 10.
> Shaffer fails to justify the emotional shifts in his characters. Walter's attempted suicide is melodramatic and incredible. However, there is perception in the writing. Shaffer is trying to prove that blood is thinner than water.

15  TREWIN, J. C. Review of Five Finger Exercise. Illustrated London News (2 August):200.
> Shaffer writes with a feeling for phrase demonstrated by few recent playwrights.

16  TYNAN, KENNETH. Review of Five Finger Exercise. Observer (London), 20 July, p. 13.
> Mixed-up son, ineffectual father, and domineering mother combination. Son is rebelling against his rich, philistine father. In its vacuumlike situation, it is hard to believe the desperation.

17  WALSH, MICHAEL. Review of Five Finger Exercise. Daily Express (London), 17 July, p. 5.
> A play with a merciless regard for truth, unerring flair for characterization and dialogue. Shaffer is an overnight great of the British theatre.

18  WORSLEY, T. C. "Give Me a Good Play." New Statesman 56 (26 July):112-13.
> Five Finger Exercise is a good "good play" with nothing particularly original about its subjects, characters, or

1959

milieu, but Shaffer's writing brings it all new life.

19     \_\_\_\_\_. Review of <u>Five Finger Exercise</u>. <u>Financial Times</u>
    (London), 17 July, p. 13.
       Very favorable toward the play.


<u>1959</u>

1 ANON. "Family Portrait." Long Island <u>Newsday</u>, 9 December,
    p. 7c.
       A favorable review of <u>Five Finger Exercise</u>.

2 ANON. "<u>Five Finger Exercise</u>: Re-interpretation of a Fine
    Play." <u>Times</u> (London), 22 September, p. 13.
       On the new London production, after the original cast
    moved to Broadway.

3 ANON. Review of <u>Five Finger Exercise</u>. <u>Time</u> (14 December):
    77.
       Shaffer can write sharp dialogue and create atmosphere,
    tension, and characterization.

4 ASTON, FRANK. "<u>Five Finger Exercise</u> Subtle and Substantial."
    New York <u>World-Telegram and The Sun</u>, 3 December; <u>New York
    Theatre Critics' Reviews</u>, p. 208.
       Each character has a chance to make a long speech of
    exposition, analysis, and comment. A good, tough show.
    Smashing.

5 ATKINSON, BROOKS. "Family Affairs: Peter Shaffer's <u>Five
    Finger Exercise</u> Has Been Staged by John Gielgud." <u>New
    York Times</u>, 13 December, sec. 2, p. 3.
       Reports on the "conspicuous success" of <u>Five Finger
    Exercise</u> in London and of the London <u>Evening Standard</u>
    Award to Peter Shaffer as the most promising British
    playwright of 1958. The title of <u>Five Finger Exercise</u>
    suggests a carefully planned piano composition. A well-
    made play; the writing is immaculate. It is a "gem of
    civilized theatre."

6     \_\_\_\_\_. "<u>Five Finger Exercise</u>: Music Box Presents a Study
    of Britons." <u>New York Times</u>, 3 December, p. 45; <u>New York
    Theatre Critics' Reviews</u>, p. 210.
       Precise prose, no gaudy phrases, and subtle characteri-
    zation. A perfect cameo, the result of underwriting and
    underacting in the best sense.

7  BEAUFORT, JOHN. Review of <u>Five Finger Exercise</u>. <u>Christian Science Monitor</u>, 5 December, p. 14.
   An expert piece of dramatic craftsmanship. Cruelties inflicted by the failure to communicate, to understand, and truly to love.

8  BOLTON, WHITNEY. "Engrossing, Adult British Import." New York <u>Morning Telegraph</u>, 4 December, p. 2.
   "Adult, painstaking and engrossing theatre."

9  BRISSON, FREDERICK. "Importing Foreign Drama: <u>Five Finger Exercise</u> Crosses the Atlantic." <u>Theatre</u> (December):24–25.
   <u>Five Finger Exercise</u> crosses local barriers without difficulty because of its universal appeal. Shaffer made changes in the script for the American production in order to avoid linguistic difficulties.

10  _____. Preface to <u>Five Finger Exercise</u>. New York: Harcourt, Brace & Co., pp. 5–7.
   Brisson, who coproduced <u>Five Finger Exercise</u> on Broadway, sees the play as variations on the theme of misunderstood personality: the powerlessness to communicate one's emotional needs to another. The seemingly simple play has many interwoven elements and, like a Bach piano piece, is enormously complicated. Shaffer is "articulate, meticulously honest, and endowed with a fine theatrical awareness." He reveals his characters as starkly as Ibsen, as elliptically as Turgenev, and as hopefully as Barrie.

11  CHAPMAN, JOHN. "<u>Five Finger Exercise</u> a Doodle." New York <u>Daily News</u>, 3 December; <u>New York Theatre Critics' Reviews</u>, p. 209.
   "A stylish example of theatrical doodling," with not much to it. Intelligently written, but fails to strike a major chord.

12  CLURMAN, HAROLD. Review of <u>Five Finger Exercise</u>. <u>Nation</u> (16 May):461–63.
   New material presented in an old mold. Technically glib, with pleasant humor and quips. Neat explanations; eloquent but self-conscious editorializing.

13  _____. Review of <u>Five Finger Exercise</u>. <u>Nation</u> (19 December): 475–76.
   Something forced and false in each crucial plot turn, either for effective curtains or to make its point. A gentler version than Osborne's about what is making men in England angry. Shaffer will grow as a playwright when he

1959

frees himself from the conventional English theatrical
forms and feelings.  An advance for British drama.
[Shaffer was deliberately working with conventional British
forms in order to get the spectators to follow him into
his play.  (See Part I 1960.9.)]

14  COLEMAN, ROBERT.  "Five Finger Exercise Thrilling."  New York
      Daily Mirror, 3 December; New York Theatre Critics' Re-
      views, p. 210.
         Brilliant theater and an absorbing study of the problem
      of communication between the generations, such as the
      jealousy between mother and daughter over Walter.

15  COOKE, RICHARD P.  Review of Five Finger Exercise.  Wall
      Street Journal, 4 December, p. 12.
         Five Finger Exercise has style and wit and is tightly
      written, but not of the glib neatness of the true "well-
      made play."

16  DASH, THOMAS R.  "Five Finger Exercise an Impressive British
      Import."  Women's Wear Daily, 3 December, p. 60.
         Shaffer can be grouped with John Osborne and Anthony
      Creighton as another angry, young playwright, but less
      turbulent than the other two.  A profound dissection of
      warped relationships.  The ending is perhaps nebulous and
      inconclusive, but this is a synthesis of life and does not
      follow precise, geometrical equations.

17  _____.  "Five Finger Exercise in London."  Women's Wear Daily,
      14 August, p. 21.
         A probing and revealing drama that deserves its ac-
      colades, even if it does augur more violence than it
      delivers.

18  FIELD, ROWLAND.  "Five Finger Exercise Is Triumphant Per-
      formance."  Newark Evening News, 3 December, p. 58.
         "Wonderful play of extraordinary lucidity and perfect
      performing."  "Vibrant drama of personal tensions and
      heart and mind conflict."

19  HEWES, HENRY.  "Oedipus Wrecks."  Saturday Review (19 Decem-
      ber):24.
         At its center, Five Finger Exercise is a triangle among
      mother, son, and tutor, and about the eventual escape of
      the son from his oedipal relationship.  Shaffer is a
      talented writer, but the audience feels little compassion
      for the victims.

20  HIPP, EDWARD SOTHERN. Review of Five Finger Exercise. Newark
    Sunday News, 6 December, sec. 3, p. E6.
        A tingling drama in a fascinating style of writing,
    which is subdued and marked by its economy of words. "A
    touch of distinction" on Broadway.

21  HOBE. Review of Five Finger Exercise. Variety, 9 December,
    p. 70.
        Even better on Broadway than in London. Shaffer's
    thesis:  hate-filled, human relationships are destructive.
    Shaffer should have had Walter die to be true to his
    thesis.

22  KERR, WALTER. Review of Five Finger Exercise. New York
    Herald Tribune, 3 December; New York Theatre Critics' Re-
    views, p. 209.
        It is Shaffer's special virtue that he can take a stage
    full of withdrawn and obtuse characters and make them in-
    teresting to watch because he has been able to find the
    blind spot that makes each character ignorant of the
    others.

23  LEWIS, EMORY. Review of Five Finger Exercise. Cue (12
    December):9.
        Slight and not very satisfying play; civilized and in-
    telligent, but a bit dull. Shaffer has promise, and once
    he gets the family probing out of his system, he may have
    good scripts to offer.

24  LITTLE, STUART W. "Briton Wrote New Scene to Open His Play
    in New York." New York Herald Tribune, 8 December, p. 21.
        Shaffer on the difference between British and American
    audiences and on the American theater in general.
    Tennessee Williams, whose plays are poetic and violent, is
    the American playwright he most admires.

25  LOFTUS, JOSEPH A. "Playwright's Moral Exercise." New York
    Times, 29 November, sec. 2, pp. 1, 3.
        Quotes Shaffer on the meaning of Five Finger Exercise:
    "a morally based play, . . . concerned with various levels
    of dishonesty--the cruel lie and the motiveless lie. The
    play seems to be unresolved because it is about the fabric
    of life, which is continuous." As for the title and con-
    ception of the play, one day Shaffer, whose hobby is piano,
    "picked up a book labeled 'Five Finger Exercise'. . . for
    the exercise of five interrelated elements and how they
    react to one another and how they strengthen each other,
    or weaken each other, if you use them wrong." The London

1959

>     newspaper critics voted it the Best Play by a New Play-
>     wright for the 1958-1959 season.

26  McCLAIN, JOHN.  "Top-Draw Import With Sterling Cast."  New
    York Journal American, 3 December; New York Theatre Critics'
    Reviews, p. 207.
>         Theme of Five Finger Exercise is the inability of
>     people to unburden themselves honestly to one another.
>     Great theater.

27  REUTER.  "N.Y. Welcome for London Play."  Times (London), 4
    December, p. 15.
>         Cites rave reviews of Five Finger Exercise in New York.

28  TYNAN, KENNETH.  Review of Five Finger Exercise.  New Yorker
    (12 December):100-2.
>         Five people in need of love, each one seeking it where
>     it is least likely to be forthcoming.  Shaffer exposes the
>     pain and rage that ensue when one human being ignores
>     another's plea for sympathy.  Play of mutual incomprehen-
>     sion.  The pieces are perfectly interlocking, but the
>     audience will be unmoved because of the "bloodlessness" of
>     the writing.  Shaffer builds up to emotional climaxes, but
>     lacks the verbal felicity to achieve them.  Favorable com-
>     parisons between Five Finger Exercise and Swiss watches,
>     chess problems, and Inge's A Loss of Roses, and an un-
>     favorable comparison with Turgenev's A Month in the
>     Country.  (See Part I 1961.2.)

29  WATTS, RICHARD, Jr.  "A Powerful New Play from England."  New
    York Post, 3 December; New York Theatre Critics' Reviews,
    p. 208.
>         A glowing review of Five Finger Exercise which credits
>     Walter with showing Shaffer's deftest and wisest sense of
>     characterization.

30  _____.  "The Power of Five Finger Exercise."  New York Post,
    13 December, p. 13.
>         Shaffer is the most talented of the new crop of British
>     playwrights, and his first efforts have produced a very
>     fine play.

31  WEBB, W. L.  "Committed to Nothing But the Theatre."  Man-
    chester Guardian, 27 August, p. 4.
>         The beauty of Five Finger Exercise is the result in
>     part of Shaffer's "pure, almost intellectual passion for
>     the theatre."  The play is remarkably fluent and well
>     constructed.

## 1960

1 ANON. "Critics Choose Five Finger Exercise." Times (London), 21 April, p. 16.
   Named Best Foreign Play of the 1959-1960 New York theater season.

2 ANON. "Five Finger Exercise." Theatre (January):18-19.
   Two pages of photographs from the New York production of the play, which is about the powerlessness to communicate emotional needs to others.

3 ANON. "One Family Split Four Ways." Life (21 March):93-94.
   A very favorable review of Five Finger Exercise.

4 ANON. "A Playwright's Twisty Road toward Success." Life (21 March):97.
   Notes on Shaffer's life and a statement by the playwright on playwriting: "You ought to be able to quote six lines when you leave the theater."

5 BALCH, JACK. Review of Five Finger Exercise. Theatre Arts (February):14-16.
   A dissection of evil; a sprightly flow of dialogue in a play of great force.

6 DRIVER, TOM F. "Drama Wanted: Fresh Air." Christian Century (6 January):15-16.
   Five Finger Exercise is believable, but the spectator does not know why the uninteresting plot or unimportant ideas should concern him. No plot and no suspense, in fact, after the first fifteen minutes, all the audiences can ask is, "So what?"

7 HAYES, RICHARD. Review of Five Finger Exercise. Commonweal (1 January):395.
   "The queerest divertisement of serious assumption on the Broadway scene." More than plausible, moral doodling; it offers interest to the ear, if not quite to the mind.

8 LEWIS, THEOPHILUS. Review of Five Finger Exercise. America 102 (9 January):428.
   A favorable review of Five Finger Exercise, as a Freudian drama of incestuous desires.

9 ROSS, DON. "Peter Shaffer Is an Enemy of 'Togetherness.'" New York Herald Tribune, 3 January, sec. 4, p. 3.
   Biographical details about and quotations by Shaffer on

1960

the British theater in general and his own in particular.
Shaffer considers Elizabethan drama great because it
treated private and personal problems; one of the problems
with the modern English stage is that it avoids those
problems. In Five Finger Exercise, Shaffer uses the stock
properties of the boring family plays that the British
love, so that the audience will feel solid ground under its
feet and follow the playwright into his play.

10  SHAFFER, PETER. "Labels Aren't for Playwrights." Theatre
Arts (February):20-21.
An early interview with Shaffer, in which he reveals
that he hopes to write many different kinds of plays and
does not want to be labeled as a writer of "week-end-
cottage naturalism," or anything else for that matter.

11  VIDAL, GORE. "Strangers at Breakfast." Reporter 22 (7
January):36-37.
The Harringtons of Five Finger Exercise as an "anti-
family" of stereotypes and strangers with nothing in com-
mon, forced by blood to share the same house. Sees the
theme of the play as the demise of the Western family.

12  WHITTAKER, HERBERT. "Direction Defeats an Old Cliche."
Globe and Mail (London), 2 January, p. 10.
Five Finger Exercise proves that a play that was successful in London can also be so on Broadway, even when it
is a domestic drama.


1961

1  SHAFFER, PETER. "Five Finger Exercise." Theatre Arts
(February):27-56.
The play in published form and notes on Shaffer's life.

2  TYNAN, KENNETH. Curtains: Selections from the Drama Criticism and Related Writings. New York: Atheneum, pp. 335-
37.
Contains a reprint of the review of Five Finger Exercise
which originally appeared in the New Yorker. (See Part I
1959.28.)


1962

1  ANON. "Mr. Peter Shaffer's Two Stories." Times (London),
15 February, p. 8.

1962

Announcement of the first performance of The Private
Ear and The Public Eye in Cambridge on 9 April 1962. The
production was entitled "Two Stories."

2 ANON. Observer (London), 6 May, p. 27.
Short biographical sketch of Shaffer.

3 ANON. "Variations on a Triangle: Evening of Skill in Enter-
tainment." Times (London), 11 May, p. 12.
Not very favorable review of The Private Ear and The
Public Eye. Shaffer has diluted the social impact of Five
Finger Exercise, "as if not to disturb."

4 DARLINGTON, W. A. Review of The Private Ear and The Public
Eye. Daily Telegraph (London), 11 May, p. 16.
The Public Eye is sophisticated, artificial comedy.
Clever and very funny. The Private Ear is a gem of
writing.

5 GASCOIGNE, BAMBER. Review of The Private Ear and The Public
Eye. Spectator (18 May):653.
The Private Ear is slight and humorous, without becoming
condescending or callous. The Public Eye is a brilliantly
serious piece of fantasy.

6 GELLERT, ROGER. "Encircling Gloom." New Statesman 63 (18
May):732.
Both The Private Ear and The Public Eye are deeply
flawed.

7 HOBSON, HAROLD. Review of The Private Ear and The Public Eye.
Christian Science Monitor, 12 May, p. 4.
Favorable towards both plays, which have the human
understanding of Five Finger Exercise. The Public Eye is
the "sure-fire hit."

8 KEOWN, ERIC. Review of The Private Ear and The Public Eye.
Punch (16 May):768.
Calls Shaffer one of England's major playwrights, of a
kind that is badly needed.

9 KRETZMER, HERBERT. Review of The Private Ear and The Public
Eye. Daily Express (London), 12 May, p. 7.
The sexual battleground, where dreams are corrupted and
turned into rubble. Writing that seldom falters. Both
pieces are extremely well made, but The Public Eye is intended to be the more important work.

1962

10  LAMBERT, J. W.  Introduction to <u>Five Finger Exercise</u>.  In <u>New English Dramatists</u>.  Vol. 4.  Edited by Tom Maschler.  Harmondsworth, England:  Penguin Books, pp. 9-10; 169-256.
    Includes the text of and brief comments on the play.

11  SHULMAN, MILTON.  Review of <u>The Private Ear</u> and <u>The Public Eye</u>.  <u>Evening Standard</u> (London), 11 May, p. 21.
    The battle of the sexes:  the fog that men find themselves in when they try to understand women.  <u>The Private Ear</u> is about sensitivity versus obtuseness.  <u>The Public Eye</u> is the less successful piece because it is not sure of its fantasy or its reality; too loquacious and sometimes too close to a review sketch, but funny and telling.  Works of wit coupled with an exuberant affection for words.

12  TREWIN, J. C.  Review of <u>The Private Ear</u> and <u>The Public Eye</u>.  <u>Illustrated London News</u> (26 May):860.
    <u>The Public Eye</u> should not be analyzed, just taken for the wonderful fantasy that it is; <u>The Private Ear</u> is the better of the two pieces.  Shaffer is an exceptionally understanding dramatist.

13  TYNAN, KENNETH.  "London Can Keep It."  <u>Observer</u> (London), 13 May, p. 25.
    In <u>The Private Ear</u>, Shaffer makes the mistake of trying to write about a class lower than his own.  <u>The Public Eye</u> is the better play because Shaffer is not trying to exhibit a mastery of lower class idiom which he does not have; its "free flow of linguistic fantasy" saves the evening.

14  WORSLEY, T. C.  Review of <u>The Private Ear</u> and <u>The Public Eye</u>.  <u>Financial Times</u> (London), 11 May, p. 26.
    Severe criticism of plays that want for a sense of "real life."  <u>The Private Ear</u> lacks shape, coherence, and mood; the characters are puppets manipulated for effects.  <u>The Public Eye</u> lacks coherence and cohesion.  The audience enjoys the plays more than the critic does.

## 1963

1  ANON.  "Love Antic and Frantic."  <u>Time</u> (18 October):76, 78.
    <u>The Private Ear</u> and <u>The Public Eye</u> "defy the laws of mental gravity and lift a playgoer out of his world only to see it better. . . ."  <u>The Public Eye</u> has the edge in "freshness and invention."  Love in marriage is content not form:  the sharing of experiences rather than the bandying

of words.  The Private Ear, despite its technical adroit-
ness, seldom breaks free of the "anticlimatic act of the
expected."

2  ANON.  "New Cast Alter Emphasis . . . The Private Ear and The
     Public Eye."  Times (London), 10 September, p. 13.
        With a new cast, The Private Ear is much better than
     before.  There is no improvement in The Public Eye, de-
     spite Shaffer's "elegantly elaborate speeches."

3  ANON.  "Pantomine by Stealth . . . 'The Merry Roosters'
     Panto.'"  Times (London), 20 December, p. 5.
        Retelling of the Cinderella story, with music and
     lyrics (by Stanley Meyers and Steven Vinaver).  The ideas
     are often brilliant, even if they expire before they have
     established themselves theatrically.

4  ANON.  "Peter Shaffer's Personal 'Dialogue.'"  New York Times,
     6 October, sec. 2, pp. 1, 3.
        An interview with Peter Shaffer on the theater, reli-
     gion, and ritual.

5  ANON.  Review of The Private Ear and The Public Eye.  News-
     week (21 October):104.
        Short circuits in human communication.  Cranking out
     endless words, Shaffer says we communicate better without
     them.  The reviewer has nothing good to say about the
     plays.

6  ANON.  Review of "The Merry Roosters' Panto."  Observer
     (London), 22 December, p. 14.
        Blurb in the theater section:  "Private and progressive
     jokes may deter some parents, but plenty of audience
     participation for non-political children."

7  BOLTON, WHITNEY.  "London-versus-N.Y. Comparisons of Shaffer
     Plays Are Invidious."  New York Morning Telegraph, 14
     October, p. 2.
        Both The Private Ear and The Public Eye are enchanting.

8  _____.  "Private Ear and The Public Eye Enchanting, Superbly
     Cast."  New York Morning Telegraph, 11 October, p. 2.
        "Unequivocal joy, the purest pleasure, the soundest
     entertainment" of the season.  Shaffer writes in a
     "heavenly, smooth and persuasive way."

9  CHAPMAN, JOHN.  "Private Ear and Public Eye Are Irresistible
     English Comedies."  New York Daily News, 10 October; New

1963

York Theatre Critics' Reviews, p. 249.
Silky-smooth, literate, and artful, witty, and irre-
sistibly human.

10  CHRISTIANSEN, RICHARD.  Review of The Private Ear and The
Public Eye.  Chicago Daily News, 11 December, p. 79.
A happy combination of substance and style in two con-
trasting yet complementary comedies about romantic love.

11  CLURMAN, HAROLD.  Review of The Private Ear and The Public
Eye.  Nation (9 November):305-6.
Shaffer is a playwright-in-progress, on his way from
Terence Rattigan to assuming his own identity.  The reward
of Shaffer's craftsmanship is that depth and suggestion of
larger issues exist even in what seems to be slight
material.

12  COLBY, ETHEL.  "Two One-Act Plays Latest Fine Import from
Britain."  Journal of Commerce, 10 October, p. 6.
Both plays are scintillating, witty, and tightly
assembled.

13  COLEMAN, ROBERT.  "Eye-Ear Delightful Imports."  New York
Mirror, 10 October; New York Theatre Critics' Review,
p. 248.
Remarkable tour-de-force.  Entertainment for sophisti-
cates, the carriage and Rolls-Royce set.

14  COOKE, RICHARD P.  Review of The Private Ear and The Public
Eye.  Wall Street Journal, 11 October, p. 12.
Both are comedies of a high order.

15  DARLINGTON, W. A.  Review of "The Merry Roosters' Panto."
Daily Telegraph (London), 20 December, p. 13.
A show very acceptable for children.

16  DASH, TOM.  Review of The Private Ear and The Public Eye.
Show Business (2 February):2.
A delectable pair for sustained merriment; shrewdly
written and insightful.

17  GASSNER, JOHN.  Review of The Private Ear and The Public Eye.
Educational Theatre Journal 15 (December):361-62.
Two expertly fashioned plays; excellent construction,
bright and fluid dialogue.  But both exist too much on the
surface:  there is no profundity of observation, no in-
cisiveness of humor, no symbolism or mystery.  The Private
Ear is rather slight, and The Public Eye is patently con-

trived and self-consciously cute.

18  GAVER, JACK. "Shaffer Takes up a Cause." New York <u>Morning</u>
    <u>Telegraph</u>, 5 November, p. 2.
        In <u>The Public Eye</u>, Shaffer refreshingly tells the
    world that there is too much communication; and in <u>The</u>
    <u>Private Ear</u>, there is the thematic thread of people trying
    to make over others in their own images.

19  _____. "Silence Is Playwright's Golden Rule." Newark <u>Sunday</u>
    <u>Star-Ledger</u>, 10 November, sec. 2, p. 6.
        Shaffer on the need for noncommunication in his comments
    on <u>The Public Eye</u>.

20  GOTTFRIED, MARTIN. Review of <u>The Private Ear</u> and <u>The Public</u>
    <u>Eye</u>. <u>Women's Wear Daily</u>, 10 October, p. 36.
        Very impressed with <u>The Private Ear</u>, but finds <u>The</u>
    <u>Public Eye</u> "a very talky, very static play that drones
    away at its delicacy." Both are strong plays with Shaffer's
    individual creativity and private sensitivity.

21  HEWES, HENRY. Review of <u>The Private Ear</u> and <u>The Public Eye</u>.
    <u>Saturday Review</u> (26 October):32.
        Entertaining and delightful, although somewhat slight
    and frivolous. <u>The Private Ear</u> is a delicious, theatrical
    confection.

22  HIPP, EDWARD SOTHERN. "Shaffer Serves Double Treat." <u>Newark</u>
    <u>Evening News</u>, 10 October, p. 70.
        Wry fun and heartache with equal skill.

23  HOBE. Review of <u>The Private Ear</u> and <u>The Public Eye</u>. <u>Variety</u>,
    16 October, p. 54.
        Impressed with this "sparkling entertainment."

24  HOFFMAN, LEONARD. Review of <u>The Private Ear</u> and <u>The Public</u>
    <u>Eye</u>. <u>Hollywood Reporter</u>, 10 October, p. 3.
        The best plays of their kind since <u>Separate Tables</u>.
    Shaffer captures each character with the flick of a pen,
    and each twist has a Chekhovian quality about it.

25  HOPE-WALLACE, PHILIP. Review of "The Merry Roosters' Panto."
    <u>Manchester Guardian</u>, 20 December, p. 7.
        A spirited little show.

26  HUGHES, ELINOR. "The Brains behind the 'Eye' and 'Ear.'"
    <u>Boston Sunday Herald</u>, 29 September, sec. 4, p. 3.
        Shaffer on the need to rewrite a play based on its

963

intended audience as well as for the actors who will be performing it.

27  KERR, WALTER.  "Magic over Matter."  New York <u>Herald Tribune</u>, 27 October, mag., p. 25.
      A noncommittal review of <u>The Private Ear</u> and <u>The Public Eye</u>.

28  _____.  Review of <u>The Private Ear</u> and <u>The Public Eye</u>.  New York <u>Herald Tribune</u>, 10 October; <u>New York Theatre Critics' Reviews</u>, pp. 249–50.
      Sight inventions; deftly contrived and cheerfully entertaining.

29  KRETZMER, HERBERT.  Review of "The Merry Roosters' Panto." <u>Daily Express</u> (London), 20 December, p. 4.
      Identifies Shaffer's purpose in the play:  Why <u>should</u> Cinderella go to the ball?  Has she <u>earned</u> the rights of leisure?

30  LAPOLE, NICK.  "S-Men Try for Another Broadway Hit."  New York <u>Journal-American</u>, 6 October, p. 23L.
      A theater piece of ideas and strong characterization will be produced in New York by Roger L. Stevens.  [On <u>The Private Ear</u> and <u>The Public Eye</u>.]

31  LEWIS, ALLAN.  Review of <u>The Private Ear</u> and <u>The Public Eye</u>. <u>Sunday Herald</u>, 27 October, p. 18.
      Both plays are brilliantly written.  <u>The Public Eye</u> is a gem; a combination of whimsy and realism, and far superior to <u>Five Finger Exercise</u>.  Shaffer is original enough to deal with conventional material and make it fresh and bright.

32  LEWIS, EMORY.  Review of <u>The Private Ear</u> and <u>The Public Eye</u>. <u>Cue</u> (19 October):28.
      Two little comedies sparkling with wicked wit and sure insight into modern social foibles.  <u>The Private Ear</u> is the more pensive piece; <u>The Public Eye</u> is more vivacious. Shaffer beautifully blends wit and pathos; meticulously observed and superbly orchestrated.  Nuance here is a fine art.

33  LEWIS, THEOPHILUS.  Review of <u>The Private Ear</u> and <u>The Public Eye</u>.  <u>America</u> (7 December):752–53.
      <u>The Private Ear</u> is a delectable vignette of life; a story of gentle disillusionment.  In <u>The Public Eye</u>, the dialogue varies from brilliant to incandescent.

20

34 McCARTEN, JOHN. Review of The Private Ear and The Public Eye.
New Yorker (19 October):99-100.
The Private Ear is bothersome. The Public Eye has a
quota of wit; it is a trifle, but enjoyable.

35 McCLAIN, JOHN. "An Import--But Why?" New York Journal American, 10 October; New York Theatre Critics' Reviews, p.
250.
Shaffer has a gift for dialogue, a sense of the ridicu-
lous, and a message of sorts. The Private Ear has charm,
compulsion, and humor; but The Public Eye is longwinded,
and what promised to be a delightful romance, vanished.

36 NADEL, NORMAN. "Emotions Gently Laid Bare in Shaffer's The
Public Eye and The Private Ear." New York World-Telegram
and The Sun, 10 October, p. 19.
Shaffer is a "rare playwright who has uncontested ac-
cess to the intimate feelings of the people he observes,
and writes about." The Public Eye is the stronger of the
two plays.

37 OPPENHEIMER, GEORGE. "1-Acter Plus 1-Acter May Add Up to
Long Run." Long Island Newsday, 10 October, p. 2c.
Likes both plays, with a preference for The Private Ear.

38 PEET, CREIGHTON. "A Couple of Humorous 'Privates.'" Norfolk
Virginia-Pilot, 20 October, p. F-7.
The Private Ear and The Public Eye are sheer delights,
and just what the Broadway season had been lacking.

39 PREE, BARRY. "Peter Shaffer Interviewed by Barry Pree."
Transatlantic Review (Autumn):62-66.
An interview which took place in 1963, after the production of The Private Ear and The Public Eye and before
that of The Royal Hunt of the Sun. (Also see Part I
1971.4.)

40 PRIDEAUX, TOM. "[Broadway's] Best and Brightest Season in a
Decade." Life (22 November):38.
Picture of and caption on The Private Ear and The Public
Eye, the most polished high-comedy writing in many years.
Warmth, tenderness, and wise sympathy for the fumbling
ways of man.

41 SHULMAN, MILTON. Review of "The Merry Roosters' Panto."
Evening Standard (London), 20 December, p. 4.
Slapstick but sophisticated parody, which is more for
adults' taste than for children's.

1963

42  SMITH, MICHAEL.  Review of The Private Ear and The Public Eye.
    Village Voice, 17 October, pp. 10, 14.
        The ragged edges of The Private Ear suggest that Shaffer
    was attempting to transcend his material, and his "equi-
    vocal attitude toward his characters suggests a temptation
    toward the adventure of self-exploration."  The Public Eye
    is hilarious but trivial and probably better as a short
    story than as a play.

43  TAUBMAN, HOWARD.  "The Private Ear and The Public Eye Open."
    New York Times, 10 October, p. 51; New York Theatre
    Critics' Reviews, p. 251.
        The Private Ear is a trifling anecdote spun out for an
    hour; written cleverly and disarmingly, but commonplace
    at the core.  The Public Eye is wise and sophisticated
    high comedy:  it soars.

44  WATTS, RICHARD, Jr.  "Two Delightful London Comedies."  New
    York Post, 10 October; New York Theatre Critics' Reviews,
    p. 251.
        Acknowledges Shaffer's gift for witty urbanity and
    skill in drawing characters and recognizes the winning
    quality of humor, sympathy, and imagination in The Private
    Ear and The Public Eye.

45  WORSLEY, T. C.  Review of "The Merry Roosters' Panto."
    Financial Times (London), 20 December, p. 18.
        A dismal failure.  Spares Shaffer the embarrassment by
    not even mentioning his name.


                            1964

1  "Artaud for Artaud's Sake."  Encore 11 (May–June):20–31.
        Edited transcript of a discussion on the Theater of
    Cruelty among Peter Brook, Peter Hall, Peter Shaffer, and
    Michel St-Denis.  Artaud's theater is the point of depar-
    ture for a more general discussion of the stage, past and
    present.  Shaffer presented the following ideas:  The
    theater attempts to produce "repeatability," and the play-
    wright's problem is to find words that will have much the
    same vitalizing effect every time they are spoken which
    requires great poetry; the psychological drama is not
    dead:  it has hardly begun; the last version of a play is
    written in rehearsal:  a text that is not changed during
    rehearsals is a dead one.

2  ANON.  "London Diary."  Evening Standard (London), 8 July,

1964

p. 6.
Shaffer calls The Royal Hunt of the Sun, which was five
years in the writing, "a spirited autobiography." His
motive was to restore spectacle to the theater (along with
spirituality and intellect). The first draft was historical, but it became more and more an expression of man's
hopes and fears for the world. Shaffer is planning a
charade about modern life in which ten people will play
three parts each.

3   ANON. "Stage Challenge to Production . . . The Royal Hunt of
     the Sun." Times (London), 9 December, p. 9.
        More concerned with the production than with the
     writing, the weaknesses of which become more evident with
     familiarity.

4   BARKER, FELIX. "A Young Man's Dazzling Success." Evening
     News (London), 12 September, [page number not available].
        In the whole history of pageant drama no other has been
     so ambitious as The Royal Hunt of the Sun, nor has any
     other spectacle so touched the historical imagination.

5   BRIEN, ALAN. "Silent Epic--with Words." Sunday Telegraph
     (London), 13 December, p. 12.
        Themes are on a heroic scale; Shaffer's language gets
     flattened under the load of themes and pageantry in The
     Royal Hunt of the Sun.

6   BRYDEN, RONALD. Review of The Royal Hunt of the Sun. New
     Statesman (17 July):95-96.
        A good, conventional chronicle play, strides ahead of
     what Shaffer has done before; but Shaffer is no poet. The
     play proper is all contained in the second act.

7   DARLINGTON, W. A. Review of The Royal Hunt of the Sun. Daily
     Telegraph (London), 9 December, p. 18.
        The philosophy is too tightly packed to be followed
     easily. Thanks to fine performances, act 2 works in spite
     of Shaffer's writing.

8   GASCOIGNE, BAMBER. "All the Riches of the Incas." Observer
     (London), 12 July, p. 24.
        Review of The Royal Hunt of the Sun. Shaffer's richest
     writing to date makes for sheer aural pleasure, especially
     in the descriptive passages. Unfortunately, there are
     moments when the philsophy gets the upper hand. The cen-
     tral question is the agnostic's search for something that
     can take the sting out of death; suspects that Shaffer is

1964

looking for the same answer.

9  GILLIATT, PENELOPE. "A Huge Stride Backwards--with the Inca."
    Observer (London), 13 December, p. 24.
       The writing reduces The Royal Hunt of the Sun to the
    level of a pageant play; there is very little theatrical
    energy or intellectual content in the text.

10 GROSS, JOHN. "Amazing Reductions." Encounter 23, no. 3:50.
       The Royal Hunt of the Sun is less complex and inventive
    than Shaffer's domestic plays. Much is just straight-
    forward chronicle play framed by a rudimentary narrative.

11 HOBSON, HAROLD. "In Search of Bliss." Sunday Times (London),
    13 December, p. 25.
       The Royal Hunt of the Sun supports the fallacies of the
    Noble Savage and the message that man's perfect condition
    is that of poetic and benevolent communism. Believes that
    Shaffer is saying that if Atahuallpa was not resurrected
    Jesus could not have been either, and that that is false
    logic.

12 _____. "Royal Hunt of the Sun Acclaimed." Christian Science
    Monitor, 15 December, p. 5.
       In this quality play, Shaffer is not attacking Chris-
    tianity, just expressing disbelief in resurrection.

13 KINGSTON, JEREMY. Review of The Royal Hunt of the Sun.
    Punch(15 July):99.
       A major theater event:  it stands alone among modern
    plays for visual beauty and excitement.  Pizarro's role is
    of heroic stature.  The "dialectic arguments" against
    Christianity and about man's search for time are the only
    defects.

14 LAMBERT, J. W.  Review of The Royal Hunt of the Sun.
    Christian Science Monitor, 11 July, p. 6.
       It is a joy to behold a play that dares to touch the
    immensities.

15 LEVIN, BERNARD. "Thank You Mr S for the Greatest Play in My
    Lifetime." Daily Mail (London), 9 December, [page number
    not available].
       Concludes after three viewings of The Royal Hunt of the
    Sun that "no greater play has been written and produced in
    our language in my lifetime."

16 M., E. C. "Rhetoric But Ordinary Philosophical Content."

1964

Stage and Television Today (London), 9 July, p. 23.
Hopes that Shaffer has now gotten epic drama out of his
system and will go back to writing his "wonderfully observed comedies."

17  MYRO.  Review of The Royal Hunt of the Sun.  Variety, 16
December, p. 64.
Majestic command of language in "one of the great
theatrical contributions of our time."

18  NIGHTINGALE, BENEDICT.  Review of The Royal Hunt of the Sun.
Manchester Guardian, 8 July, p. 7.
Shaffer's abilities are slimmer than his vast ambition
in the muddled and essentially hollow play.  No original-
ity of ideas or feeling for characters except as the pro-
jection of ideas.

19  PRYCE-JONES, ALAN.  Review of The Private Ear and The Public
Eye.  Theatre Arts (January):65-66.
A favorable review, which finds The Public Eye to be of
a higher level of farce, but The Private Ear of more real
interest.

20  ROBERTS, PETER.  "After the Fanfare . . ."  Plays and Players
(September):26-28.
Review of the Chichester Festival season, at which The
Royal Hunt of the Sun was presented.  Compares Shaffer's
epic drama to Shaw's Saint Joan.

21  RUTHERFORD, MALCOLM.  "The Christ that Died."  Spectator (17
July):82, 84.
The Royal Hunt of the Sun is a play with a hole in the
middle, and the spectacle cannot conceal it.  It lacks
characters and language of its own.  Pizarro has worldly
skill and knowledge, but he is empty and he is the biggest
defect in the play; Atahuallpa knows the secret of living.
An epic that signifies nothing.  The confrontations do not
take place, and the themes are so momentous that there is
no language for them.  But something so ambitious should
not be allowed to fail.

22  SHAFFER, PETER.  "In Search of a God."  Plays and Players
(October):22.
Contains the first act of The Royal Hunt of the Sun and
Shaffer's statement on the meaning of his play:  an in-
tense, obscure relationship between two men, one of whom
is the prisoner of the other, and each of whom mirrors the
other.  Act 2 of The Royal Hunt of the Sun appears in the

1964

November 1964 issue.

23  SHORTER, ERIC. Review of The Royal Hunt of the Sun. Daily
      Telegraph (London), 8 July, p. 16.
         Documentary on Spain's conquest of the Incas and a
      study of man's immortal longings; the two themes do not
      always coalesce.

24  SHULMAN, MILTON. Review of The Royal Hunt of the Sun. Even-
      ing Standard (London), 8 July, p. 4.
         Epic theater in the grand manner. Shaffer's play is of
      considerable intellectual and dramatic merit, but should
      be cut by twenty minutes.

25  _____. Review of The Royal Hunt of the Sun. Evening Standard
      (London), 9 December, p. 14.
         Intensity, maturity, and intelligence of Shaffer's
      writing give the ultraromantic events urgency and relevance.
      Argument is secondary to the production by John Dexter and
      Desmond O'Donovan.

26  TAYLOR, JOHN RUSSELL. "Shaffer and the Incas." Plays and
      Players (April):12-13.
         Shaffer gives background information on The Royal Hunt
      of the Sun and comments on his other plays in an interview
      with John Russell Taylor. The Royal Hunt of the Sun is
      the result of Shaffer's having read William H. Prescott's
      monumental History of the Conquest of Peru during a period
      of confined bedrest.
         There was a third play for the bill which contained The
      Private Ear and The Public Eye which Shaffer does not name,
      but which he considers the best of the three.

27  TREWIN, J. C. Review of The Royal Hunt of the Sun. Illus-
      trated London News (8 August):208.
         The writing does not match the production. Trewin
      wishes that The Royal Hunt of the Sun had been written by
      Marlowe, who would have found the heroic mode. Acknowl-
      edges that Shaffer is an ambitious and technically accom-
      plished writer.

28  WATTS, RICHARD, Jr. "Peter Shaffer's Historical Drama." New
      York Post, 9 August, p. 18.
         A beautifully written drama that combines history with
      philosophical speculation. A brilliant and powerful play
      of distinction and importance, but not the masterpiece of
      the century.

29  YOUNG, B. A. "Chichester Views New Shaffer Play." New York
Times, 8 July, p. 40.
    As a spectacle The Royal Hunt of the Sun is superb, but
it lacks depth (though not importance) of argument. As
much pageant as play. Definitely on the credit side of
the National Theatre's activities.

30  _____. Review of The Royal Hunt of the Sun. Financial Times
(London), 8 July, p. 24.
    The Royal Hunt of the Sun is about honor: Pizarro can-
not break his word to Atahuallpa because he realizes that
they are two of a kind. Techniques are thrown in with
almost insolent boldness. Some moments of truly great
theatrical genius and diabolically effective invention,
but short on beauty of language and profundity.

## 1965

1  ANON. "British Plays Modified for Broadway." Times (London),
31 December, p. 13.
    The Royal Hunt of the Sun is better in New York than in
London. Re-creation of the spectacular effects, but the
text has been trimmed a bit, the philosophical diatribes
between Pizarro and Atahuallpa abbreviated, and the production is better for it.

2  ANON. "Hunting Heaven." Newsweek (8 November):96.
    The Royal Hunt of the Sun tries to be too "total":
historical, psychological, and moral; it is vigorous, un-
certain, exciting, disappointing, lucid, and confused, but
clearly on the side of the angels.

3  ANON. "Total Darkness Lit by Brilliant Gags." Times (London),
28 July, p. 14.
    Brilliant gags with stock characters in Black Comedy.

4  BARKER, FELIX. Review of Black Comedy. Evening News (London),
28 July, [page number not available].
    A slender revue sketch that has been given enough ideas
to keep it from sagging.

5  BENJAMIN, PHILIP. "Chichester Views Play by Shaffer." New
York Times, 29 July, p. 19.
    The situation of total darkness in Black Comedy is
based on a dueling scene in Chinese classical theater.

6  BOLTON, WHITNEY. "Grand Opera Techniques in 2 Plays." New

1965

York <u>Morning Telegraph</u>, 1 November, p. 3.
<u>The Royal Hunt of the Sun</u> verges on opera in its choral
and balletic moments (in the duo between Pizarro and
Atahuallpa, and in the ascent of the Andes).

7 _____. "<u>Royal Hunt</u> Is a Play of Beauty and Spectacle." New
York <u>Morning Telegraph</u>, 28 October, p. 3.
Eloquent, thoughtful, and masterful dramatization of the
quest for man's conscience. Act 2 is a magnificently
written treatment of good and evil.

8 BRUSTEIN, ROBERT. "Familiar Peru, Exotic Brooklyn." <u>New
Republic</u> 153 (27 November):45-46.
Without spectacular theatricality <u>The Royal Hunt of the
Sun</u> amounts to little. Total theater but fractional drama
about a fraternal romance between Atahuallpa and Pizarro.
"Being exposed to Peter Shaffer's meditations on religion,
love, life and death for three solid hours is rather like
being trapped in a particularily active wind tunnel with
no hope of egress." "Underneath the tumult and the swirl
lie a very conventional set of liberal notions about the
noble savage, the ignoble Catholic, and the way brotherly
love can bridge the gulf that separates cultures." (See
Part I 1969.2.)

9 BRYDEN, RONALD. Review of <u>Black Comedy</u>. <u>New Statesman</u> (6
August):194-95.
Shaffer has stretched a revue-sketch idea into a cast-
iron mechanism for amateurs and repertory companies. It
has laughs, but that is all.

10 CHAPIN, LOUIS. Review of <u>The Royal Hunt of the Sun</u>. <u>Christian
Science Monitor</u>, 30 November, p. 4.
Beautifully written, but needs to be tightened up.

11 CHAPMAN, JOHN. "<u>Royal Hunt of the Sun</u> a Lovely Play." New
York <u>Sunday News</u>, 7 November, sec. 2, p. 3.
Shaffer has achieved all that he had hoped for in <u>The
Royal Hunt of the Sun</u>: "theatrical writing at its beauti-
fied best" as well as "total theatre." Easily Shaffer's
most impressive play.

12 _____. "<u>The Royal Hunt of the Sun</u> Fills The ANTA Theatre
with Beauty." New York <u>Daily News</u>, 27 October; <u>New York
Theatre Critics' Reviews</u>, p. 296.
Praises Shaffer's use of language in this beautiful
play.

13  CHIARI, J. <u>Landmarks of Contemporary Drama</u>. London: Herbert
    Jenkins, pp. 210-11.
        In the chapter of "Concluding Remarks," praises <u>Five</u>
    <u>Finger Exercise</u> as an "excellent piece of naturalistic and
    probably autobiographical cannibalism which has a well-
    deserved success." Shows disdain for <u>The Royal Hunt of</u>
    <u>the Sun</u>, as Shaffer's attempt at epic drama which suffers
    from shallowness of ideas and lack of characterization,
    not to mention failure of the pseudo-poetical language.
    Finds Shaffer generally deficient in his poetic imagina-
    tion and his command of language.

14  CLURMAN, HAROLD. Review of <u>The Royal Hunt of the Sun</u>. <u>Nation</u>
    (22 November):397-98.
        The pleasure, if any, in the play is visual. The
    writing is sufficient for telling the story, but there is
    a basic hollowness in the play. It will satisfy audiences
    hungry for a semblance of theater, but is being mistaken
    for a good play . . . even for a masterpiece.

15  COOKE, RICHARD P. Review of <u>The Royal Hunt of the Sun</u>. <u>Wall</u>
    <u>Street Journal</u>, 28 October, p. 16.
        An ornate and bizarre pageant, which gains stature only
    in the final confrontation between Pizarro and Atahuallpa.
    Shaffer's insights are interesting and at times moving.
    A play worthy of respect, despite its shortcomings.

16  DARLINGTON, W. A. Review of <u>Black Comedy</u>. <u>Daily Telegraph</u>
    (London), 28 July, p. 16.
        At the Chichester Festival, <u>Black Comedy</u> is sure-fire
    funny.

17  ESSLIN, MARTIN. "All in the Text." <u>Plays and Players</u>
    (February):34.
        All else aside, <u>The Royal Hunt of the Sun</u> has a first-
    rate text, and the last scene is great and memorable.

18  FROST, DAVID. Review of <u>Black Comedy</u>. <u>Punch</u> (4 August):174-
    75.
        Shaffer's lightest work to date. Meticulously orches-
    trated, broad farce.

19  FUNKE, PHYLLIS. "A Playwright in a Hurry." <u>Louisville</u>
    <u>Courier-Journal</u>, 7 November, [page number not available].
        Background information on Shaffer's theater as well as
    on his ideas about playwriting and patriotism.

20  GELB, BARBARA. ". . . And Its Author." <u>New York Times</u>, 14

1965

November, sec. 2, pp. 1, 2, 4.
Biographical information, in which Shaffer mentions a play-in-progress called "The Coronation Mass."

21  GOTTFRIED, MARTIN.  Review of The Royal Hunt of the Sun.
Women's Wear Daily, 27 October, p. 55.
A "very ceremonial, very ritualistic, very spectacular bore. . . ."  Shaffer became over absorbed with theories and tools and forgot that it is art that matters.  Basic incompatibility between the story and the style.  Shaffer's messages are platitudinous; the historical elements drone along in commonplace pseudo-epic language; the narrator is monotonous; and the use of pure theater elements produce an untheatrical event with no stage excitement.

22  HERING, DORIS.  Review of The Royal Hunt of the Sun.  Dance Magazine (December):138-39.
Concerned with the movement and visual spectacle of the production of this grandly structured play.

23  HEWES, HENRY.  "Inca Doings."  Saturday Review (13 November): 71.
The Royal Hunt of the Sun is the season's most thrilling, most imaginative, and most beautiful event.  Less impressive as literature.  [Shaffer never intended that it be literature.]

24  _____.  "Unsentimental Journeys."  Saturday Review (29 May): 31.
The Royal Hunt of the Sun is written with "penetrating insight" rather than "showy grandiosity."  Along the way, Shaffer touches the essence that underlies historical events.

25  HIPP, EDWARD SOTHERN.  "A Conquest Missed by the Historians."  Review of The Royal Hunt of the Sun.  Newark Evening News, 7 November, pp. E1, E6.
"A vibrant entertainment, written with consummate skill . . . ," lyrical grace, and a stunning sense of pageantry.  Rare theatrical excitement in the climactic scene.

26  _____.  "New Version of Conquest."  Newark Evening News, 27 October, p. 48.
An exhilarating experience to hear literate English beautifully spoken.  Brings drama and pageantry back to Broadway despite overwriting and some static scenes.

1965

27  HOBE. Review of The Royal Hunt of the Sun. Variety, 3 Novem-
      ber, p. 60.
        Shaffer's writing starts slowly and takes undue time for
      setting the atmosphere and getting to the meat of the drama.
      The speeches are talky, and the play is heavy going for
      entertainment seekers. [However, in general, he seems to
      like the play.]

28  HOBSON, HAROLD. "Riot of Laughter." Christian Science Moni-
      tor, 4 August, p. 4.
        It has been many years since England has had as much
      laughter on her stage as with Black Comedy. A side-split-
      ting farce based on such a simple idea.

29  HOPE-WALLACE, PHILIP. Review of Black Comedy. Manchester
      Guardian, 28 July, p. 7.
        Production is an uproarious piece of slapstick vaude-
      ville, but the play itself is a trifle.

30  KERR, WALTER. Review of The Royal Hunt of the Sun. New York
      Herald Tribune, 27 October; New York Theatre Critics' Re-
      views, pp. 294-95.
        The first half of The Royal Hunt of the Sun is plainly
      without momentum; in the second half, Pizarro and Atahuallpa
      play out games of transposed identity. Only the final
      scenes demand the real attention of the audience. Nothing
      good to say about Shaffer's writing.

31  KRETZMER, HERBERT. Review of Black Comedy. Daily Express
      (London), 28 July, [page number not available].
        Rave review of the original production of Black Comedy
      at the Chichester Festival.

32  LAPOLE, NICK. "Pizarro Invades Broadway." New York Journal-
      American, 24 October, p. 23L.
        On some of the technical problems of staging The Royal
      Hunt of the Sun.

33  LEVIN, BERNARD. "Out of the Darkness a Blind Farce." Daily
      Mail (London), 28 July, [page number not available].
        Shaffer is the most diversified of the postwar play-
      wrights. Black Comedy is constructed on the most meticu-
      lous, farcical pattern. It is just a bit too long.

34  LEWIS, ALLEN. American Plays and Playwrights of the Contem-
      porary Theatre. New York: Crown Publishers, p. 258.
        Although the plays are not American, mentions briefly
      and praises The Private Ear and The Public Eye as beauti-

1965

fully written and highly ingenious.

35  LEWIS, EMORY.  Review of The Royal Hunt of the Sun.  Cue (6
        November):13.
            "Total theater," but Shaffer offers too much hollow
        rhetoric.  A worthwhile play, but not to be mistaken for
        a masterpiece; it lacks the ring of greatness.

36  LEWIS, THEOPHILUS.  "The Royal Hunt of the Sun."  America 113
        (20 November):648-49.
            Creative work in the classic mold of drama.  The finest
        of the season.

37  MAROWITZ, CHARLES.  Review of The Royal Hunt of the Sun.
        Encore 12 (March-April):44-45.
            Admires The Royal Hunt of the Sun; it is Shaffer's best
        play, although the final struggle between Pizarro and
        Atahuallpa is overwritten and overscrutinized.  Sees the
        clash of cultures as turning homosexual:  epic becomes
        "closet" drama and loses in the exchange.  (See Part I
        1973.19.)

38  MAROWITZ, CHARLES; MILNE, TOM; and HALE, OWEN, eds.  The
        Encore Reader:  A Chronicle of the New Drama.  London:
        Methuen & Co., p. 130.
            The only comment on Shaffer is a quotation attributed
        to Arnold Wesker, who allegedly said that Five Finger
        Exercise is so weak a play because it tries to place a
        Jewish mentality in Gentile clothing.

39  MARRIOTT, R. B.  Review of Black Comedy.  Stage and Television
        Today (London), 29 July, p. 13.
            A diverting trifle on truth and identity.

40  McCARTEN, JOHN.  "Gods Against God."  New Yorker (6 November):
        115-16.
            Based on evidence in The Royal Hunt of the Sun, Shaffer
        is a writer of probity, wit, skill, and imagination.  Elo-
        quent dialogue.  A completely enthralling play, after
        Pizarro and Atahuallpa meet.

41  McCLAIN, JOHN.  "Size, Style and Talent."  New York Journal
        American, 27 October; New York Theatre Critics' Reviews,
        p. 293.
            The Royal Hunt of the Sun has prolonged lapses and many
        a labored moment, but it is an effort of vast thought and
        consideration.

42  NADEL, NORMAN. "Royal Hunt a Shimmering Sunburst of Talent."
    New York World-Telegram and The Sun, 27 October; New York
    Theatre Critics' Reviews, p. 294.
        Magnificent drama, spectacle aside. Symmetry of poetry,
    noble speeches, shining strength of wisdom. The visual
    and aural effects never reduce the play to pageant. "For
    Shaffer it is a triumph. No Englishman in the century,
    save Shaw and Christopher Fry, has achieved such sensible
    beauty with words, such noble clarity of ideas. The Royal
    Hunt of the Sun might well be a masterpiece."

43  OPPENHEIMER, GEORGE. "A Playwright's Critique." Long Island
    Newsday, 6 November, 37W.
        Interview with Shaffer, specifically on The Royal Hunt
    of the Sun.

44  _____. Review of The Royal Hunt of the Sun. Long Island
    Newsday, 27 October, p. 3c.
        Poetry, drama, compassion, intellect, and above all,
    light that dazzles the eyes. Theater of ideas. Themes:
    the discovery of innocence by lust, the inability to fit
    new ideas into fanatical adherences, the failure of reli-
    gion to embrace new faiths, the sanctity of a treaty, the
    unwillingness to recognize true purity.

45  PRIDEAUX, TOM. "The Royal Hunt of Virtue." Life (10 Decem-
    ber):137-38.
        Shaffer's plays all preach the need for more compassion
    among people. In The Royal Hunt of the Sun, it is love thy
    neighbor, especially if he represents a foreign culture.

46  SHAFFER, PETER. "To See the Soul of a Man . . ." New York
    Times, 24 October, sec. 2, p. 3.
        "The neurotic allegiances of Europe, the Churches and
    flags, the armies and parties, are the villians of The
    Royal Hunt of the Sun." Its hero is "a free man, surging
    ahead under his own power." Ultimately, the play is about
    man's search for immortality.

47  SHEED, WILFRED. Review of The Royal Hunt of the Sun. Common-
    weal 83 (19 November):215-16.
        "A sad case of waste." Pizarro represents everything
    that is destructive in the old world and is ready to
    clutch at any religious and philosophical straw. Shaffer
    has written some literate lines for Pizarro, and his
    philosophy is good, sensible stuff, unpretentious and
    solid. The theme of "whoring" after immortality is so big,
    that unfortunately the play keeps getting lost in its folds.

1965

48  SHULMAN, MILTON.  Review of Black Comedy.  Evening Standard
(London), 28 July, p. 4.
A very favorable review.

49  SIMON, JOHN.  Review of The Royal Hunt of the Sun.  Hudson
Review 18 (Winter):571-74.
Looks pretentious and sounds hollow, but restores
visual illusion to the theater.

50  SMITH, MICHAEL.  Review of The Royal Hunt of the Sun.  Village
Voice, 4 November, pp. 19-20.
A disappointment, despite the language and subject
matter.  What is said is intelligent, perceptive, and
serious, but the final drama is too private.  In the character of Pizarro, Shaffer tries to write about the struggle
in Everyman's soul, but ends up writing about himself.  For
all of its shortcomings, however, the play is fascinating
to see.

51  TAUBMAN, HOWARD.  "About A Royal Hunt . . ."  New York Times,
14 November, sec. 2, p. 1.
The play is not completely successful, but it is a
courageous attempt to put life into the theater.  London
critics hailed it as a masterpiece, then condemned it as a
showy fraud; the truth lies in between.

52  _____.  "Pizarro, Gold and Ruin."  New York Times, 27 October,
p. 36; New York Theatre Critics' Reviews, p. 296.
The Royal Hunt of the Sun demonstrates Shaffer's high
intelligence and bold, imaginative reach.  Brave and daring
try, sometimes static, sometimes pretentious and arty, but
more commendable than routine ventures.  Attempts to ex-
pand the narrow horizons of theater, too often constricted
by small minds and limited imaginations.

53  TREWIN, J. C.  Review of Black Comedy.  Illustrated London
News (7 August):36.
Survives well through the first half, but should be cut.

54  WATTS, RICHARD, Jr.  "The Conqueror and the Conquered."  New
York Post, 14 November, p. 20.
Regrets having used the words "pretentiousness" and
"superficiality" in his opening night review.  The Royal
Hunt of the Sun is a tragic drama of "noble proportions
and high distinction."  (See following item.)

55  _____.  Review of The Royal Hunt of the Sun.  New York Post,
27 October, p. 83.

1966

A fascinating synthesis of the arts of the theater.
Dignified, thoughtful, and distinguished. Might be sus-
pect of pretentiousness and superficiality, but it is
absorbing drama. Does not go deeply into the conflict of
men and civilizations that Shaffer is writing about, but
it is steadily arresting. (See Part I 1965.54.)

56  YOUNG, B. A.  Review of Black Comedy.  Financial Times
    (London), 28 July, p. 22.
        Shaffer keeps the fun going.


### 1966

1  COHEN, MARSHALL.  "Theater 66."  Partisan Review (Spring):
   273-74.
       Includes a review of The Royal Hunt of the Sun, a self-
   conscious attempt to combine Artaudian mise en scène with
   the drama of ideas.

2  COHEN, NATHAN.  "Mortal Messengers on Broadway."  National
   Review (11 January):37-38.
       The production of The Royal Hunt of the Sun receives
   respect out of proportion to its content. Hollow in its
   dramatic conceptualism; vulgarized nonsense, and super-
   ficial ruminations.

3  GASSNER, JOHN.  "Broadway in Review."  Educational Theatre
   Journal 18, no. 1:57-58.
       Includes a section on The Royal Hunt of the Sun which
   explains why it does not succeed as epic drama, despite
   the best of intentions:  (1) the first half lags as drama
   and is successful only as spectacle; (2) the immortality
   whose passiveness deprives the play of the possibility of
   his passiveness deprives the play of the possibility of
   establishing a true and stirring conflict; (4) the failure
   of natives to withstand the encroachment of the Spanish
   adds up to a lack of action; (5) the author's excessive
   objectivity makes for no empathy.  (See Part I 1968.5.)

4  HOBSON, HAROLD.  "Hero of the National Theater."  Christian
   Science Monitor, 21 March, p. 4.
       After writing The Royal Hunt of the Sun and Black
   Comedy for their stage, Shaffer is the hero of the National
   Theatre.

5  NADEL, NORMAN.  "Royal Hunt Still Shining."  New York World-
   Telegram and The Sun, 9 April, p. 23.

1966

The language stirs like music. "Its prose has the soaring flight of poetry, and, at times, the grandeur of Scripture." The pageantry on stage is secondary to the play's remarkable intelligence.

6  ROGOFF, GORDON. "Richard's Himself Again:  Journey to an Actors' Theatre." Tulane Drama Review 11 (Winter):38.
    Mentions Shaffer's The Royal Hunt of the Sun and Black Comedy at the National Theatre. "England can refer confidently now to at least four young playwrights whose names were unknown ten years ago, and who show definite signs of staying--and more important--growing power:  John Osborne, Harold Pinter, Peter Shaffer, and John Arden."

7  SHULMAN, MILTON. "In the Dark--One Brilliant Joke." Evening Standard (London), 9 March, [page number not available].
    In Black Comedy, a revue sketch idea has been turned into a hilarious play.

8  TERRY, WALTER. "Grandma and the Incas." New York Herald Tribune, 23 January, mag., p. 27.
    The Royal Hunt of the Sun's beauty is in its totality of theatrical elements.

9  WINEGARTEN, RENEE. "The Anglo-Jewish Dramatist in Search of His Soul." Midstream 12 (October):40-52.
    Combines Shaffer with Pinter in questioning why modern Anglo-Jewish playwrights have nothing to say on Jewish subjects. Perhaps Shaffer did not want to have a Jewish family in Five Finger Exercise in order to avoid stereotypes. The play is unsatisfying because it seems that Shaffer had not resolved a "subconscious tension pulling the dramatist in two different directions at once." Speculates on Shaffer's debt to Artaud in the creation of The Royal Hunt of the Sun, whose language is pedestrian and whose text is "would-be poetic." Tries to find Jewish attitudes on the part of the playwright (i.e., sympathy for the underdog; the Jewish concept of messianism). Concludes that Pinter and Shaffer "are subconsciously drawing upon a vein of feeling which, as one might expect, is in part peculiar to their Anglo-Jewish experience."

1967

1  ANON.  Review of Black Comedy and White Lies.  Time (17 February):70.
    Black Comedy:  unflaggingly funny drawing-room farce;

compulsively amusing. In White Lies, Shaffer is wise
rather than clever about loners and loneliness. Black
Comedy saves the evening.

2  BARNES, CLIVE.  "Amiable Black Comedy Succeeds in Its Aim of
   Providing Simple Entertainment." New York Times, 19 October, p. 58.
        Black Comedy is "machine-made but skillful, and more
   successful than The Royal Hunt of the Sun (the "Verdi
   opera without Verdi music").  An explosively funny tour-
   de-force, without a thought in its head.  White Lies is a
   rather labored piece, a sob-stuff trifle.

3  BENEDICTUS, DAVID.  Review of The Royal Hunt of the Sun.
   Plays and Players (February):22.
        It tells of the days when there were still some good,
   brave causes left; but man was unworthy of them.  Overwhelming drama.

4  BOLTON, WHITNEY.  Review of Black Comedy and White Lies.
   New York Morning Telegraph, 14 February, p. 3.
        Finds White Lies "interesting" and loves Black Comedy,
   even if it is ten minutes too long.

5  BUNCE, ALAN N.  Review of Black Comedy and White Lies.
   Christian Science Monitor, 27 February, p. 4.
        A favorable review.

6  CHAPMAN, JOHN.  "Peter Shaffer's Black Comedies a Splendid
   Theatrical Evening."  New York Daily News, 13 February;
   New York Theatre Critics' Reviews, p. 371.
        Wit, imagination, and irrepressible laughter.  A very
   enthusiastic review.

7  _____.  "Peter Shaffer's Surprises."  New York Sunday News,
   19 February, p. S3.
        All of Shaffer's plays show literary skill, imagination,
   and a keen theatrical sense.  In the program of Black
   Comedy, Shaffer observed:  "People go to the theatre for
   man reasons, but mainly, I think, to be surprised."  White
   Lies is written with great skill.  Black Comedy is a tour-
   de-force--or farce.

8  CLURMAN, HAROLD.  Review of Black Comedy and White Lies.
   Nation (27 February):285-86.
        Black Comedy has no plot and no message; it is devoid
   of intellectual significance and too long, but very good
   "sport."  The content of White Lies is trite, but Black

1967

Comedy redeems the evening.

9  COOKE, RICHARD P.  "Shaffer Strikes Again."  Wall Street
   Journal, 14 February; New York Theatre Critics' Reviews,
   p. 372.
       A very favorable review of Black Comedy, a play in
   which there is not a trace of black humor.

10 GOTTFRIED, MARTIN.  Review of Black Comedy.  Women's Wear
   Daily, 13 February; New York Theatre Critics' Reviews,
   p. 371.
       Enthusiastic, with reservation, about Black Comedy.
   White Lies is thin and stretched too far toward sensi-
   tivity, with little redeeming theatrical value.

11 GUSSOW, MEL.  "Shedding No Light."  Newsweek (20 February):
   102-3.
       Black Comedy is enjoyable for fifteen minutes, but the
   dialogue is thin.  White Lies is langorous storytelling.

12 HEWES, HENRY.  "When You're Having More Than One."  Saturday
   Review (25 February):59.
       Black Comedy, the season's most risable romp, is per-
   haps an implied criticism of social hypocrisy.  White Lies
   is a slow-going fragment.

13 HIPP, EDWARD SOTHERN.  Review of Black Comedy and White Lies.
   Newark Evening News, 13 February, p. 20.
       Favorable towards both plays.

14 HIRSCH, SAMUEL.  "English Playwright Finds New York Is His
   Real Home."  Boston Herald, 11 January, p. C 33.
       Biographical information on Shaffer and some of his
   ideas about the theater.

15 JEFFERYS [sic], ALLAN.  Review of Black Comedy and White Lies.
   WABC-TV (12 February).
       White Lies is overlong, but Black Comedy is "the wild-
   est, wackiest piece of merriment Broadway has seen in
   years [and] the most creative, ingenious and funniest show
   of the season."

16 KERNODLE, GEORGE R.  Invitation to the Theatre.  New York:
   Harcourt, Brace & World, pp. 53, 227.
       Comments on The Royal Hunt of the Sun as a personal
   tragedy in epic form and an excellent example of epic
   theater.  Unfortunately, the achievement is an empty one.
   (See Part I 1971.1.)

17 KERR, WALTER. "In Black (Comedy) and White (Lies)." New York Times, 26 February, sec. 2, p. 1.
Theater-pieces, as opposed to plays; they occupy a stage rather than anyone's thoughts.

18 _____. "Vaudeville Variations on Chinese Theme." New York Times, 13 February, p. 42; New York Theatre Critics' Reviews, pp. 373-74.
Peter Shaffer knows his craft; he writes for actors, and he can be funny. But he is a sort of manufacturer's writer: he fabricates instead of feeling his way. Sometimes he fabricates feelings. His work seems made-up rather than imagined and the material is small and stretched. When the Chinese mimes act as if in total darkness, it is an infinitely refined form of art; with Shaffer it is pratfalls, easy boffs, and tricks. More and more of the same one-line joke; good, but long. White Lies is much more in earnest. The situation is arresting, but the play turns into a homily consisting mostly of Advice to the Loveless. We tell ourselves lies in order to avoid love; the eyes of love make us see what we are, and that scares us.

19 KLEIN, STEWART. Review of Black Comedy and White Lies. WNEW-Radio (New York), (12 February).
Black Comedy is a wildly mad farce with a painfully weak script. White Lies is a wordy character study.

20 LEWIS, EMORY. Review of Black Comedy and White Lies. Cue (25 February):8.
Enchanted evening of loony laughter. Deals with the masks we wear, our public and private images; our illusions or false cards of identity. Not profound, but clever.

21 LONEY, GLENN. "Broadway and Off-Broadway Supplement." Educational Theatre Journal 19 (May):201.
Black Comedy is the current high point in comic drama.

22 LUMLEY, FREDERICK. New Trends in Twentieth Century Drama: A Survey since Ibsen and Shaw. New York: Oxford University Press, pp. 279-83.
The brief section on Shaffer contains general comments on Five Finger Exercise, The Royal Hunt of the Sun, The Public Eye, and Black Comedy. The Royal Hunt of the Sun had to wait for six years, passing from management to management, until the subsidized National Theatre could budget for it. The result is a theatrical event, but for Shaffer's lack of the necessary power of language at his

1967

command, it is not a masterpiece.

23  McCARTEN, JOHN.  "Chinese Kookie."  New Yorker (25 February):
    91.
         Black Comedy lacks metaphysical speculations.  White
    Lies is very slight and goes on much too long.

24  MESSINA, MATT.  "Peter Shaffer's TV Script Shelved by CBS
    Playhouse."  New York Daily News, 29 July, p. 10.
         The play that Shaffer wrote about a "middle-aged
    Englishman who has a bitter-sweet liaison with a swinging
    young American cutie" will not be presented.  [No title
    is given.]

25  MORGAN, DEREK.  "Mixed Bag from Britain."  Reporter (9 March):
    50, 52.
         Enthusiastic about Black Comedy, but not so about White
    Lies: "shambling and corny."

26  NADEL, NORMAN.  "Hilarity Never Stops for Black Comedy."  New
    York World Journal Tribune, 13 February; New York Theatre
    Critics' Reviews, p. 373.
         Raves about Black Comedy.  White Lies is a "good little
    play."

27  OPPENHEIMER, GEORGE.  "Black Comedy Opens on Broadway."  Long
    Island Newsday, 13 February, p. 2A.
         Shaffer is a fine writer of dialogue, but Black Comedy
    is a bit too long and "not up to Mr. Shaffer's high stan-
    dard of comedy."

28  PRIDEAUX, TOM.  "Things That Go Bump in the Dark."  Life (10
    March):70A–70D.
         On the difficulties of acting in Black Comedy, as if
    in total darkness.

29  RICHARDSON, JACK.  "British Imports on Broadway."  Commentary
    (June):74–75.
         Black Comedy and White Lies are entirely common pieces
    of theater, not particularly good and not particularly
    bad.  Black Comedy is reminiscent of the dramas of the
    1930s and 1940s, before the class struggle and continental
    philosophy settled on the British mind.

30  SMITH, MICHAEL.  Review of Black Comedy and White Lies.
    Village Voice, 16 February, p. 21.
         White Lies is "contrived, trite, and pretentious."
    Sophie suffers from Shaffer's "didactic urge."  Black

Comedy is hilarious, but that's not enough to sustain it.
Five Finger Exercise is still Shaffer's best play; as his
plays become modern, they also lose "soul." Shaffer
should listen more to his feelings and less to his ideas.

31  TAYLOR, JOHN RUSSELL. The Rise and Fall of the Well-Made
    Play. New York: Hill & Wang, p. 162.
        In the last chapter of the book, Taylor makes the most
    casual comment on Five Finger Exercise: a very "well-
    made" play.

32  WATTS, RICHARD, Jr. "Comedy of Light in Darkness." New York
    Post, 13 February; New York Theatre Critics' Reviews,
    p. 372.
        Black Comedy is good, but long. Interesting character
    study in White Lies, which is also too long. Shaffer is a
    brilliantly versatile dramatist."

33  _____. "Peter Shaffer's Play Revisited." New York Post,
    14 September, p. 57.
        On a second viewing, White Lies seems underrated. What
    seemed overly long on opening night, now appears to be
    surprisingly moving, perceptive, and touching.

34  _____. "The Versatility of Peter Shaffer." New York Post,
    25 February, p. 20.
        Black Comedy, brilliant and uproarious tour-de-force.
    White Lies, striking and effective character study which
    starts to run down at the halfway mark. They could use
    editorial cutting. Praise for Five Finger Exercise, The
    Public Eye, The Private Ear, and The Royal Hunt of the Sun.

35  WELLWORTH, GEORGE. The Theater of Protest and Paradox:
    Developments in the Avant-Garde Drama. 3d printing. New
    York: New York University Press, p. 254. [1st printing
    1964.]
        Wellworth's inclusion of Shaffer is limited to the
    remark that Five Finger Exercise is an example of a play,
    in which a dramatist tries to exorcise his drab, middle-
    class background by denigrating it.

36  WEST, ANTHONY. "Black Comedy Enormously Funny." Vogue (15
    March):54.
        An enormously funny piece that will probably last as
    long as the theater can use comedy. A joyful harlequinade
    that is a milestone in the history of comedy. Should not
    be missed.

1968

<u>1968</u>

1  ANON.  "Shaffer's Ambitions."  <u>Times</u> (London), 21 February,
   p. 10.
        On Shaffer's talents in the theater and with music.

2  [BRIEN, ALAN.]  Review of <u>The White Liars</u>.  <u>Sunday Telegraph</u>
   (London), 25 February, [page number not available].
        <u>The White Liars</u> is a puzzling play:  it is intelligent,
   sensitively written, meticulously shaped, and full of insight; but at the same time it is cold, unmoving, and un-
   convincing.

3  BRYDEN, RONALD.  "Red-nosed Revival."  <u>Observer</u> (London),
   25 February, p. 26.
        <u>Black Comedy</u> is more at home on Shaftesbury Avenue than
   at the National Theatre, and <u>The White Liars</u> is "imper-
   fectly adapted to the stage."

4  FRENCH, PHILIP.  "Surprise, Surprise."  <u>New Statesman</u> (1
   March):279.
        At Chichester, <u>Black Comedy</u> was a beautifully balletic
   farce, but now on the West End (via Broadway) it has been
   through a coarsening process.  <u>The White Liars</u> is more
   appropriate on a television series than in the theater and
   falls below expectation for Shaffer.

5  GASSNER, JOHN.  Review.  In <u>Dramatic Soundings:  Evaluations
   and Retractions Culled from Thirty Years of Dramatic
   Criticism</u>.  Edited by Glenn Loney.  New York:  Crown Pub-
   lishers, pp. 609-11.
        Reprint of his review of <u>The Royal Hunt of the Sun</u>, in
   the chapter "A Brace of English Imports (March, 1966)."
   (See Part I 1966.3.)

6  HOPE-WALLACE, PHILIP.  Review of <u>Black Comedy</u> and <u>The White
   Liars</u>.  <u>Manchester Guardian</u>, 22 February, p. 6.
        <u>The White Liars</u> is a study in loneliness in the seedy,
   Tennessee Williams style.  <u>Black Comedy</u>:  not good, not
   bad.

7  KINGSTON, JEREMY.  Review of <u>Black Comedy</u> and <u>The White Liars</u>.
   <u>Punch</u> (28 February):319.
        In <u>Black Comedy</u>, Shaffer is an expert in the art of
   developing a situation for a roar of laughter, although
   it is hard to sustain the joke for the length of the play.
   <u>White Liars</u> tugs at the heart.

Peter Shaffer

*Peter Shaffer*

8  KRETZMER, HERBERT. Review of Black Comedy and The White Liars. Daily Express (London), 22 February, p. 3.
    The White Liars is more than a curtain-raiser; it is a beautiful idea. Black Comedy is cruder in its direction than at the National Theatre, but still brilliant.

9  LEWIS, PETER. "Black and White Brilliance." Daily Mail (London), 22 February, [page number not available].
    An evening of brilliance that establishes Peter Shaffer as one of the most brilliant theatrical conjurors. Shaffer's fault in The White Liars is to be too clever.

10 RICH. Review of Black Comedy and The White Liars. Variety, 13 March, p. 75.
    Black Comedy: a rollicking if overlong bit of fun; The White Liars: a contrived anecdote.

11 SAY, ROSEMARY. Review of Black Comedy. Sunday Telegraph (London), 25 February, [page number not available].
    Black Comedy remains "one of the most hilarious displays of pure comic invention ever seen on any stage."

12 SHORTER, ERIC. "Comedy of 'Images' is Overstrained." Daily Telegraph (London), 22 February, p. 19.
    The White Liars is pretentious and eager to moralize. "Images" are strained to the breaking point.

13 SHULMAN, MILTON. Review of Black Comedy. Evening Standard (London), 22 February, p. 4.
    Still fresh in its new production.

14 T., J. R. Review of Black Comedy and The White Liars. Times (London), 22 February, p. 13.
    Shaffer was blessed with the sort of idea that wrote itself in Black Comedy, a "dazzlingly adroit piece of comic plotting." The White Liars, on the other hand, is not much of a play, just a "frail, wispy little piece."

1969

1  ANON. "Peter Shaffer's New 'Battle' for Olivier-Gielgud." Variety, 3 September, p. 63.
    Peter Shaffer has submitted "The Battle of Shrivings" to the National Theatre; John Gielgud and Laurence Olivier may be starred.

2  BRUSTEIN, ROBERT. The Third Theatre. New York: Alfred A.

43

1969

Knopf, pp. 114–16.
Contains an essay entitled "Peru in New York: The Royal Hunt of the Sun by Peter Shaffer"--a reprint. (See Part I 1965.8.)

3 CHAGRIN, CLAUDE. "French Dressing: Claude Chagrin Talks to Sheridan Morley about Mime and Movement." Plays and Players (March):52–53.
Morley arranged the mime and movement for The Royal Hunt of the Sun at the National Theatre and on Broadway. Photograph of a scene from the play.

4 COHN, RUBY. Currents in Contemporary Drama. Bloomington and London: Indiana University Press, pp. 124–25.
A comment on Shaffer in the context of modern British drama and a comment on The Royal Hunt of the Sun, whose succession of spectacular scenes does not add up to a coherent drama.

5 ESSLIN, MARTIN. Reflections: Essays on Modern Theatre. Garden City, NY: Doubleday & Co., p. 85.
The chapter "Brecht and the English Theatre" suggests that Shaffer wrote The Royal Hunt of the Sun at the request of Peter Hall for the Royal Shakespeare Company.

6 GASSNER, JOHN, and QUINN, EDWARD, eds. The Reader's Encyclopedia of World Drama. New York: Thomas Y. Crowell, pp. 759–60.
Notes on Shaffer's life and plays through Black Comedy.

7 KNAPP, BETTINA L. Antonin Artaud: Man of Vision. New York: David Lewis, p. 202.
Artaud declared that La Conquête du Mexique was to be his best example so far of Theater of Cruelty, with themes of man's desire to colonize, his need to brutalize his fellow man, his right to convert natives to Christianity. He wanted to dramatize events, not men. "Peter Schaffer's [sic] The Royal Hunt of the Sun is, in my opinion, a virtual transposition of Artaud's metaphysical drama The Conquest of Mexico."

8 RICHARDS, STANLEY, ed. Modern Short Comedies from Broadway and London. New York: Random House, pp. 7–69.
Contains the text of Black Comedy as well as notes on Shaffer's life.

9 SALEM, DANIEL. La Révolution théâtrale actuelle en Angleterre. Paris: Denoël, pp. 132–35.

Cursory remarks on Five Finger Exercise, The Royal Hunt of the Sun, Black Comedy, and on Shaffer the man. Shaffer refused to allow The Royal Hunt of the Sun to be performed in South Africa because the segregation laws did not permit black and white actors on the same stage; Shaffer wanted blacks to play the Incas.

10 TAYLOR, JOHN RUSSELL. Anger and After: A Guide to the New British Drama. London: Methuen & Co., pp. 272-78. (Also The Angry Theatre: New British Drama. New York: Hill & Wang.)

The most interesting quality of Shaffer's work is its impersonality, with the classical qualities of the traditional dramatist: cast-iron construction; a coherent and well-plotted story; solid, realistic characterization; extreme fluency in the composition of lively, speakable, exactly placed dialogue. But ultimately, Shaffer emerges as mysterious and as impalpable as Walter in Five Finger Exercise (one of the most chilly and enigmatic heroes ever). The Royal Hunt of the Sun has a rather heavy, self-conscious script, but is highly respectable, intelligent, and well-written.

*11 WEISE, WOLF-DIETRICH. Chapter 7. In Die "Neuen" englischen Dramatiker in ihrem Verhältuis zu Brecht. Vol. 3. Bad Homberg: Frankfurter Beiträge zur Anglistik und Amerikanistic.

Listed in Schultz (Part I 1976.21).

## 1970

1 ANON. Review of "The Battle of Shrivings." Time (30 March): 77.

"A Shaw play without Shaw." Lacks sufficient toughness and passion.

2 BAIL. Review of "The Battle of Shrivings." Variety, 11 February, p. 61.

Magnetic and occasionally profound, but falters from inherent incredibility. An attempt on the grand scale which lacks Shaw's wit. Raises questions that go without answers.

3 BARKER, FELIX. Review of "The Battle of Shrivings." Evening News (London), 6 February, [page number not available].

The clash between theoretical idealism and practical evil. Unduly long and shrouded in symbolism.

1970

4  BRYDEN, RONALD.  Review of "The Battle of Shrivings."
      Observer (London), 8 February, p. 31.
         Nothing good to say about the play.  Shaffer cannot
      handle his material this time.

5  EDWARD, SYDNEY.  "What the Riots Did to Peter Shaffer."
      Evening Standard (London), 9 January, pp. 20-21.
         Shaffer was never more involved in any play than in
      "The Battle of Shrivings," due to the effect of having
      been in America at the time he was writing it.  The riots
      at Columbia University were a major starting point for
      his play.  Reports that Shaffer's next play will involve
      the Faust legend.

6  FRENCH, PHILIP.  Review of "The Battle of Shrivings."  Plays
      and Players (March):20, 21, 59.
         Intellectual melodrama, which does not hold together.
      England's most self-conscious and articulate student of
      theatrical forms superimposed the ideological framework of
      The Royal Hunt of the Sun on the domestic situation of
      Five Finger Exercise.  But "The Battle of Shrivings" does
      not achieve the synthesis that gave The Royal Hunt of the
      Sun its power or the purity of accomplishment of Five
      Finger Exercise, Black Comedy, The Private Ear and The
      Public Eye.

7  HAYMAN, RONALD.  "Like a Woman They Keep Going Back To."
      Drama (Autumn):60-62.
         On selected, post-1956 British playwrights.  The re-
      marks on Shaffer are more general than profound.

8  HOBSON, HAROLD.  "Gielgud, Shaffer, and Hall--Had a Great
      Fall."  Christian Science Monitor, 13 February, p. 6.
         What Shaffer tried to write about in "The Battle of
      Shrivings" is outside the reach of his tiny hand.

9  _____.  Review of "The Battle of Shrivings."  Sunday Times
      (London), 8 February, p. 53.
         "Endless acres of rarified absurdities blown over by
      windy suspirations of coarse breath."  A copious flow of
      big words for little ideas.

10  HOPE-WALLACE, PHILIP.  Review of "The Battle of Shrivings."
      Manchester Guardian, 6 February, p. 8.
         Serious and honorable, too long and not witty enough.
      Reversal of roles:  the saint is in despair and the de-
      stroyer is life-affirming.  The play is tough going, but
      leaves a lot to ponder.

11  KINGSTON, JEREMY.  Review of "The Battle of Shrivings."  Punch
    (11 February):236.
        The exposition is overly long, but the work is rich in
    ideas, arresting abuse, and scenes that linger in the
    mind.

12  LEWIS, PETER.  "This Truth Game Makes Us All Groggy."  Daily
    Mail (London), 5 February, [page number not available].
        What begins as an intellectual debate on the nature of
    man ends as an emotional bloodbath.  Shaffer's dialogue,
    laced with epigrams and metaphors, is the most thoughtful
    available today.

13  MARCUS, FRANK.  "Poet V. Philosopher."  Sunday Telegraph
    (London), 8 February, [page number not available].
        A work of stature, with cleverness, wit, and fine
    theatrical carpentry, but it does not bear close examina-
    tion.  Shaffer strains for significance, but it eludes
    him.

14  MARRIOTT, R. B.  "The Philosopher and the Poet Join Battle
    at Shrivings."  Stage and Television Today (London), 12
    February, p. 13.
        When Shaffer tries to be profound, he comes across as
    shallow and boring.  The characters and debate are unreal
    and unconvincing, banal and tedious.

15  NIGHTINGALE, BENEDICT.  "Some Immortal Business."  New
    Statesman (13 February):227.
        Shaffer should have stuck to emotions and left philoso-
    phy alone (i.e., he should not have written The Royal Hunt
    of the Sun and "The Battle of Shrivings").  "The Battle of
    Shrivings" is very bad.  Message:  Lux in tenebris--The
    Royal Hunt of the Sun revisited.

16  PEARSON, KENNETH.  "News in the Arts."  Sunday Times (London),
    1 February, p. 51.
        Both Shaffer brothers will have plays opening at about
    the same time.  [Sleuth and "The Battle of Shrivings."]
    Photographs of the Shaffer brothers together.

17  POUTEAU, JACQUES.  "New Shaffer Play Analysis of Man."
    Newark Evening News, 7 February, p. 6.
        A noncommital review of "The Battle of Shrivings."

18  RICHARDS, STANLEY, ed.  Best Plays of the Sixties.  Garden
    City, NY:  Doubleday & Co., pp. 523-624.
        Includes The Royal Hunt of the Sun as one of its

1970

selections, as well as a biographical sketch of Shaffer.

19  SHORTER, ERIC.  Review of "The Battle of Shrivings."  Daily
    Telegraph (London), 6 February, p. 16.
        Sharp intelligence of ideas.  The characters are mouth-
    pieces and do not move the critic.

20  SHULMAN, MILTON.  Review of "The Battle of Shrivings."
    Evening Standard (London), 6 February, p. 24.
        Archetypical Thinker and Artist, rather than real
    people.  Interesting literary exercise, impressed with its
    own verbal felicity and rhetoric.  Flashes of profundity,
    poetry, and wit.  Brave but flawed event.

21  TREWIN, J. C.  Review of "The Battle of Shrivings."  Illus-
    trated London News (21 February):26.
        Artificial and contrived scheme, with Shaffer's pre-
    sence behind it all.

22  WARDLE, IRVING.  "Play by Shaffer Opens in London:  'Battle
    of Shrivings' Tells of Philosopher's Plight."  New York
    Times, 7 February, p. 23.
        Well-made, traditional piece of domestic melodrama
    about human perfectability.  It fails to honor its philo-
    sophical theme.

23  _____.  Review of "The Battle of Shrivings."  Times (London),
    6 February, p. 13.
        Shaffer is concerned with the subject of human per-
    fectability, but does little justice to the theme.  The
    level of debate might have been a good deal higher.

24  YOUNG, B. A.  Review of "The Battle of Shrivings."  Financial
    Times (London), 6 February, p. 3.
        The play is just not believable.


### 1971

1  KERNODLE, GEORGE, and KERNODLE, PORTIA.  Invitation to the
   Theatre:  Brief Edition.  New York:  Harcourt Brace
   Jovanovich, pp. 58, 140-41.
       (See Part I 1967.16.)


2  LONEY, GLENN.  "Which Twin Has the Tony?:  Broadway Greets
   Twin Playwrights Peter and Tony Shaffer."  After Dark
   (April):21-23.
       A three-way conversation among the interviewer and

1973

Peter and Anthony Shaffer on games, drugs, <u>Sleuth</u>, and
"The Battle of Shrivings." Includes pictures of Peter and
Anthony Shaffer, <u>Sleuth</u>, and <u>The Royal Hunt of the Sun</u>.

3  PENNEL, CHARLES A. "The Plays of Peter Shaffer: Experiment
   in Convention." <u>Kansas Quarterly</u> 3, no. 2:100-9.
       A pioneer article on Shaffer's theater, from <u>Five</u>
   <u>Finger Exercise</u> through "The Battle of Shrivings."

4  PREE, BARRY. Interview with Peter Shaffer. In <u>Behind the</u>
   <u>Scenes: Theater and Film Interviews from the "Transat-</u>
   <u>lantic Review."</u> Edited by Joseph F. McCrindle. New York:
   Holt, Rinehart & Winston, pp. 205-10.
       A reprint. (See Part I 1963.36.)

5  TAYLOR, JOHN RUSSELL. <u>The Second Wave: British Drama for</u>
   <u>the Seventies</u>. New York: Hill & Wang, p. 11.
       Very brief mention of Shaffer in the context of his
   contemporaries (Bolt, Osborne, and Pinter).


<u>1972</u>

*1 HAMMERSCHMIDT, HILDEGARD. <u>Das historische Drama in England</u>
   <u>(1956-1971): Erscheinungsformen und Entwicklungstendenzen</u>.
   Wiesbaden and Frankfurt.
       Listed in Schultz (Part I 1976.14).

2  <u>McGraw Hill Encyclopedia of World Drama</u>. Vol. 4. New York:
   McGraw Hill, pp. 83-85.
       Biographical sketch, mention of Shaffer's plays through
   1970, and one paragraph each on <u>Five Finger Exercise</u> and
   <u>The Royal Hunt of the Sun</u>.

3  PARKER, JOHN, comp. <u>Who's Who in the Theatre: A Biographical</u>
   <u>Record of the Contemporary Stage</u>. 15th ed. London:
   Pitman & Sons, p. 1397.
       A one-paragraph biographical and professional résumé
   through 1970.


<u>1973</u>

1  BARBER, JOHN. Review of <u>Equus</u>. <u>Daily Telegraph</u> (London),
   27 July, p. 13.
       Some of the dialogue is overly literary, but Shaffer is
   a dramatic technician of high order.

1973

2  BARNES, CLIVE. "Peter Shaffer's Equus Is Box-Office Success."
   New York Times, 17 August, p. 11.
        Equus is about humanity and divinity. In the condi-
   tioning of civilization, man is losing the gods of his
   childhood innocence. Alan is the hero, and Dr. Dysart is
   the villain.

3  BILLINGTON, MICHAEL. Review of Equus. Manchester Guardian,
   27 July, p. 12.
        Like "The Battle of Shrivings" and The Royal Hunt of the
   Sun, Equus is a direct confrontation between reason and
   instinct. Better than the two former plays because here
   the intellectual argument and the poetic imagery are
   virtually indivisible. Life based on organized faith is
   usually based on some form of neurosis, but without worship
   or belief it is barren. The character of Dysart is a
   study of a man of reason, soured by the need to bottle up
   and contain his instincts. (The rectangular room represents his orderly world.) A sensationally good play in
   bold, clear, and vivid theatrical terms.

4  CHRISTIE, IAN. Review of Equus. Daily Express (London),
   27 July, p. 10.
        The production is so good that it blinds the audience
   to the fact that it is watching pretentious, philosophical
   claptrap.

5  CUSHMAN, ROBERT. Review of Equus. Observer (London), 29
   July, p. 30.
        Admires the play, although it "groans" under Dysart's
   expository passages. Realistically, Equus is a dud;
   theatrically, it is a triumph. Shaffer writes fair to indifferent prose, but imagines magnificent scenes. Observes
   similarities between Equus and The Royal Hunt of the Sun,
   and Equus and Five Finger Exercise.

6  DAVIES, RUSSELL. Review of Equus. New Statesman (3 August):
   165-66.
        More praise for the production and the acting than for
   the writing: "a mass of exposition," out of which actor
   Alex McCowen has to make a coherent whole for the part of
   Dysart.

7  DAWSON, HELEN. Review of Equus. Plays and Players (September):
   43-45.
        Glib oversimplification, shallow trendiness, and lang-
   uage that rarely rises to the lofty imagery.

8  FORD, CHRISTOPHER. "High Horse." Manchester Guardian, 6 August, p. 8.
     Background information on the actual event which inspired the writing of Equus. Someday Shaffer would like to write a play about the Faust legend; for Shaffer, the blinded Faust gets something ecstatic and positive from his transformation.

9  GILLIATT, PENELOPE. "Power-Cut Laughter." In Unholy Fools. Wits, Comics, Disturbers of Peace: Film and Theater. New York: Viking Press, pp. 190-92.
     On the production of Black Comedy at the Chichester Festival. The play seems to be a blinding idea, not very boldly pursued.

10 HAYMAN, RONALD. "John Dexter: Walking the Tightrope of Theatrical Statement." Times (London), 28 July, p. 9.
     Interview with John Dexter, who directed Equus.

11 HOBSON, HAROLD. Review of Equus. Sunday Times (London), 29 July, p. 33.
     Praise for the new play.

12 ____. "A Triumph at London's National Theater [sic]." Christian Science Monitor, 10 August, p. 14.
     Background information on the writing of Equus, "a moving and deeply profound play." Also mentions that Shaffer considered the critical reaction to "The Battle of Shrivings" unnecessarily savage, and it hurt him deeply.

13 HUGHES, CATHERINE. "London's Stars Come Out." America 129 (8 December):443-44.
     Equus is firmly conceived and vividly imagined. Shaffer's philosophy is too shallow to be entirely convincing, and the writing is a trifle pat. Shaffer is a rare playwright, in that he has something to say and that he can keep the audience continually challenged and absorbed while he is saying it.

14 KALSON, ALBERT E. Review of Equus. Educational Theatre Journal 25 (December):514-15.
     Equus "has restored passion to the theatre." Observations on similarities between Five Finger Exercise and Equus, and between The Royal Hunt of the Sun and Equus, as well as with Anthony Burgess's A Clockwork Orange and Enderby.

15 KERR, WALTER. "A Psychiatric Detective Story of Infinite

1973

Skill." <u>New York Times</u>, 2 September, sec. 2, pp. 1, 3.
Equus reanimates the spirit of mystery that makes the
stage a place of breathless discovery rather than a class-
room for rational demonstration. The theater-going public
has been looking for a craftsman like Shaffer for a long
time.

16 KINGSTON, JEREMY. Review of <u>Equus</u>. <u>Punch</u> (8 August):188.
A contest of wills between two men in which the defeat
of one involves the wreck of the other. The main features
are too meticulously crafted, too neat, to ring true;
nevertheless, Equus is a distinguished play.

17 LAMBERT, J. W. Review of <u>Equus</u>. <u>Drama</u>, no. 111 (Winter):
14-16.
Brief but thought-provoking observations on Equus as a
clash between the Apollonian or rational forces and the
Dionysian or instinctive ones. Shaffer does not treat his
theme so effectively here as in the intellectually under-
rated <u>The Royal Hunt of the Sun</u>. He is an honest, sometimes stiff, writer, but he does not attempt to disguise
his theme with rhetoric.

18 LAWSON, WAYNE PAUL. "The Dramatic Hunt: A Critical Evalua-
tion of Peter Shaffer's Plays." Ph.D. dissertation, The
Ohio State University. (<u>DAI</u> 34:7374A-75A.)
Places Shaffer within the context of contemporary
British drama and analyzes the plays from <u>Five Finger
Exercise</u> through "The Battle of Shrivings."

19 MAROWITZ, CHARLES. <u>Confessions of a Counterfeit Critic: A
London Theatre Notebook 1958-1971</u>. London: Eyre Methuen,
pp. 88-90.
Contains a reprint of his review of <u>The Royal Hunt of
the Sun</u> which originally appeared in <u>Encore</u>. (See Part I
1965.37.)

20 PIT. Review of <u>Equus</u>. <u>Variety</u>, 8 August, p. 44.
A powerful and moving philosophical drama, inconclusive
perforce, but "written with sharp intelligence and com-
passion, often witty and poetic, always challenging the
audience to think about conventional wisdom."

21 "Philip Oaks Talks to Peter Shaffer." <u>Sunday Times</u> (London),
29 July, p. 33.
An interview with Shaffer about his work and the
theater in general. Oaks quotes Shaffer as saying: "I
passionately believe that people come to the theatre to be

surprised, moved, illuminated. They're not interested
simply in what they're <u>hearing</u>. They're receiving what
you say viscerally." Shaffer believes that the theater is
"a need as basic as sex."

22  SHAFFER, PETER. "What We Owe Britten." <u>Sunday Times</u>
(London), 18 November, p. 35.
    Shaffer's praise for and indebtedness to Benjamin
Britten, the object of Shaffer's "hero worship."

23  SHULMAN, MILTON. Review of <u>Equus</u>. <u>Evening Standard</u> (London),
27 July, pp. 28-29.
    A complex, intellectual play.

24  WARDLE, IRVING. Review of <u>Equus</u>. <u>Times</u> (London), 27 July,
p. 15.
    A play about the god-like image of Equus, not about
Alan or Dysart. Very little real dialogue; mostly solilo-
quies. Shaffer's excellence comes through in Dysart's
speeches. "The Battle of Shrivings," <u>The Royal Hunt of
the Sun</u>, and <u>Equus</u> are tournaments between Apollo and
Dionysus, and Apollo always wins, even though the intent
is to celebrate the dark gods. Shaffer is a Western intellectual and cannot conjure up Dionysian, only Apollonian rules of reason and control.

25  WATTS, RICHARD, Jr. "The Boy Obsessed with Horses." <u>New
York Post</u>, 18 August, p. 16.
    A favorable review of <u>Equus</u>.

26  YOUNG, B. A. Review of <u>Equus</u>. <u>Financial Times</u> (London),
27 July, p. 3.
    A fine, thought-provoking play in every detail.


1974

1  ANON. Note on <u>Equus</u>. <u>Harper's Bazaar</u> (October):133.
    Alerts its readers to watch for <u>Equus</u>, which "promises
to be the most exciting evening in the theatre this
season."

2  BARNES, CLIVE. "<u>Equus</u> a New Success on Broadway." <u>New York
Times</u>, 25 October, p. 26; <u>New York Theatre Critics' Reviews</u>,
pp. 204-5.
    A highbrow suspense story, an essay in character and
motivation, and a journey into someone's mind. Dysart
represents the playwright coming to grips with alienation.

1974

A very fine and enthralling play, and a fresh hope for
Broadway.

3 BEAUFORD, JOHN. "Brilliant British Import: Shaffer's In-
ventive Equus Hits Broadway." Christian Science Monitor,
4 November; New York Theatre Critics' Reviews, p. 202.
A psychological mystery play, which explores the
genesis of a crime. Remarkable work.

4 BRUKENFELD, DICK. "All That Fuss about Horses?" Village
Voice, 31 October, pp. 91-92.
Did not like act 1 or its tacky conclusion, but found
that the play got better as Dysart's problems were explored
in act 2.

5 CLURMAN, HAROLD. Review of Equus. Nation (16 November):
506-7.
Something like a detective story with a message; brilliantly crafted, handsomely written, and unusually compelling. It has an air of spectacle, of theater, despite
its apparent austerity and functionalism. The philosophy
is bogus, and Dysart needs to be cured of his faulty
reasoning.

6 EICHELBAUM, STANLEY. "Crime against Horses." San Francisco
Sunday Examiner and Chronicle, 15 September, p. 12.
Though Equus is a distinctive and stageworthy piece,
the psychology is banal or far-fetched and could have
been better thought out.

7 GIFFORD, SANFORD. "A Psychoanalyst Says Nay to Equus." New
York Times, 15 December, sec. 2, p. 5.
A professor at the Harvard Medical School writes of his
bitter reaction to the play. Compares it to Freud's case
of "Little Hans," about a patient whose horse-phobia re-
presented fears of his father's sexual prohibitions.
Shaffer's restatement in the most vulgar and stereotyped
form that madness is the price of genius. Well-spaced
coups de théâtre--the boy masturbating to orgasm on a
galloping horse and a "gratuitous" nude scene. [The nudity
was John Dexter's and not Peter Shaffer's idea.] The
play is a skillful mix of truth, banality, and pretention.

8 GILL, BRENDAN. "Unhorsed." New Yorker (4 November):123-24.
Shaffer is an ingenious playwright and a superb writer
of dialogue, as evidenced by Five Finger Exercise, The
Royal Hunt of the Sun, Black Comedy, and Equus, a con-
tinually thrilling melodrama, whose message is that we

would have no need for violence if we were free to be what we really are, without having to bear the crushing weight of an identity.

9  GLENN, JULES. "Anthony and Peter Shaffer's Plays:  The Influence of Twinship on Creativity." American Imago 31: 270-92.
      Analyzes the plays of Peter and Anthony Shaffer as literature written by twins.  His thesis is that the Shaffers' plays are constructed on the premise of doubles--two characters who mirror each other.  In Equus (which receives the most thorough treatment of any of the plays), those characters are Dysart and Alan, who behave as twins in their "similarity, identification, and ambivalence." Both destroy; both are fascinated by mythology; both have sexual problems.  Uses a similar method in his approach to White Lies and The White Liars, in both of which Sophie, Baroness Lemberg, senses a kinship with one of the rock singers.  In The Public Eye, the twinship is between Belinda Sidley and Julian Cristoforou.  Pizarro and Atahuallpa in The Royal Hunt of the Sun are rivals who admire each other and become increasingly similar in the course of the drama.  [Dr. Glenn is a medical psychoanalyst.]  (See also Part II 1974.2.)

10  _____. "Twins in Disguise:  A Psychoanalytic Essay on Sleuth and The Royal Hunt of the Sun." Psychoanalytic Quarterly 43, no. 2:288-302.
      A study of the close kinship between the protagonists and of their twin traits.  The Royal Hunt of the Sun studies the sadomasochistic relationship demonstrated by Pizarro's cruel treatment of Atahuallpa.  (See also Part II 1974.3.)

11  _____. "Twins in Disguise.  II.  Content, Form and Style in Plays by Anthony and Peter Shaffer." The International Review of Psycho-Analysis 1, no. 3:373-81.
      Explores further the twin elements in Black Comedy, White Lies, The White Liars, and The Public Eye.  (See also Part II 1974.4.)

12  GOTTFRIED, MARTIN. "Equus in London." Women's Wear Daily, 16 January, p. 22.
      Senseless and obsolete Freudianism/anti-Freudianism. The writing is mundane, and the use of flashback is trite. Shaffer is a talented Naturalistic playwright who wants to write stylized plays.  [The director decided on the stylized elements.]

1974

13 \_\_\_\_\_. "Shaffer's Equus at the Plymouth." New York Post,
   25 October; New York Theatre Critics' Reviews, p. 206.
      Essentially trite and occasionally weird idea. Dexter's
   directing raises a small play to epic size. The play uses
   horseflesh passion to represent homosexuality.

14 GRUEN, JOHN. "Equus Makes Star of Peter Firth." New York
   Times, 27 October, sec. 2, pp. 1, 5.
      Some biographical information on the actor who origi-
   nated the role of Alan Strang; comments on the opposing
   demons that possess that patient and on the psychiatrist
   in the play.

15 GUSSOW, MEL. "Shaffer Details a Mind's Journey in Equus."
   New York Times, 24 October, p. 50.
      On Shaffer's background work for Equus and on his future
   projects. Quotes Shaffer as saying: "If your own thing
   is destructive and appalling, it has to be stopped."
   Shaffer is working on "a political play on rather an epic
   scale . . . a ferocious encounter in a probation office,"
   and "The Syllabub Saloon."

16 HINCHLIFFE, ARNOLD P. British Theatre 1950-70. Totowa, NJ:
   Rowman & Littlefield, p. 149.
      Space does not permit the critic to "explain why the
   Shaffer brothers were so successful in the West End."

17 HOBE. Review of Equus. Variety, 30 October, pp. 88, 90.
      Fascinating and strangely suspenseful, but finds the
   nudity [which was not Shaffer's idea] gratuitous dramati-
   cally.

18 K[ALEM], T. E. "Freudian Exorcism." Time (4 November):119-
   20; New York Theatre Critics' Reviews, pp. 205-6.
      Dubious intellectual premise. The characters came out
   of Shaffer's bag of stereotypes. With theatrical brio,
   he brings the audience in touch with his own sin, guilt,
   confession, and atonement—perhaps even redemption.

19 KAUFFMAN, STANLEY. Review of Equus. New Republic (7 December):18, 33-34.
      Equus is better than Five Finger Exercise and The Royal
   Hunt of the Sun, but not good enough. A play built from
   the end forward, so that Shaffer could neatly develop what
   was needed to fill in the gaps. The doctor's jealousy
   theme seems an afterthought. It is unbelievable that the
   one doctor in whose care Hesther Salomon would entrust
   Alan has no faith in his profession. Dysart was passion-

ate, until Shaffer took his passion away from him. [Dysart did not exist until Shaffer wrote him into existence.]

⋆ 20  KERR, WALTER. "Equus: A Play that Takes Risks and Emerges Victorious." New York Times, 3 November, p. 11.
"Equus is one of the most remarkable examples of stage-craft, as well as sustained and multifaceted sensibility that the contemporary theater has given us." A play of melodramatic tensions and designed ritual. Shaffer's craftsmanship is "as ingenious as it is legitimate."

21  KISSEL, HOWARD. "Equus: Not for the Horsey Set." Women's Wear Daily, 10 September, p. 44.
Mainly on John Dexter's direction of Equus.

22  _____. Review of Equus. Women's Wear Daily, 18 October; New York Theatre Critics' Reviews, pp. 203-4.
Eloquent, pungent, witty dialogue; stupendous theatricality. The purpose is ritual, not psychological, understanding. A theatrical event of the greatest importance.

23  KROLL, JACK. "Horse Power." Newsweek (4 November):60.
Like D. H. Lawrence's, Shaffer's horse represents the power and danger of unsublimated instincts. Dysart's is the most explosively eloquent self-pity ever witnessed on stage. Too pat in its intellectual substance, but a devilishly masterful work of craftsmanship. Pure theater at its best.

24  MOOTZ, WILLIAM. Review of Equus. Louisville (KY) Courier-Journal and Times, 15 December, p. H8.
A sensational and oddly satisfying play.

25  OPPENHEIMER, GEORGE. Review of Equus. Long Island Newsday, 10 November, pp. II9, II70.
No other playwright today has Shaffer's macabre imagination and amazing versatility.

26  PROBST, LEONARD. Review of Equus. NBC-TV (24 October); New York Theatre Critics' Reviews, p. 207.
The first act is labored; the second act is one of the best in years. More thrilling than logical; more sexy than sound. Cleverly conceived, totally gripping, and even overwhelming at the end.

27  REED, REX. "Equus: A Bad Premise, but Good Theater." New York Sunday News, 3 November, leisure sec., p. 7.
A muscularly written but disturbingly incoherent psycho-

1974

logical study, with whose premise the critic disagrees:
"a demonic liberal platitude." The play is entertaining,
but hard to take seriously.

28  SANDERS, KEVIN.  Review of Equus.  WABC-TV (30 October); New
    York Theatre Critics' Reviews, p. 207.
        A bit soupy at times, but highly literate and sophisti-
    cated, with soaring speeches.

29  SCHICKEL, RICHARD.  "Showman Shaffer."  Time (11 November):
    117, 119.
        Biographical information on Shaffer and a review of
    Equus which mentions the opening night standing ovation
    for the playwright.

30  SIMON, JOHN.  "The Blindness Is Within."  New York Magazine
    (11 November):118.
        Worn-out whimsy about the virtue of insanity.  The
    physical production is splendid, but nothing can overcome
    the hollowness within.

31  STASIO, MARILYN.  Review of Equus.  Cue (4 November):23.
        Startles the senses with images of unsettling beauty,
    as it jars the mind with discordant but provocative ideas.
    Alan's passion for horses is a metaphorical argument for
    homosexuality, but presented with elegance and forceful-
    ness.  Remarkable theatrical experience; compelling work.

32  TALLMER, JERRY.  "A Playwright's Role."  New York Post, 12
    December, p. 45.
        On Shaffer, his family, and the incident that inspired
    Equus.

33  TAYLOR, JOHN RUSSELL.  Peter Shaffer.  Writers and Their
    Work Series, no. 244.  Harlow, England:  Longman House,
    34 pp.
        An essay on Shaffer's plays; calls Equus and Black
    Comedy his most impressive achievements.

34  WATT, DOUGLAS.  "Equus A Stunner Filled with Chills, Drama,
    Psychiatry."  New York Sunday News, 3 November, leisure
    sec., p. 3.
        A thriller of the old school, brightened by intelligence
    and lively and provocative dialogue.  Powerful, exciting
    theater.

35  _____.  "Equus Is a Smashing Psycho-drama."  New York Daily
    News, 25 October; New York Theatre Critics' Reviews,

pp. 201-2.
Bargain basement psychoanalysis, but gripping theater.
Palatable and powerful entertainment.

36  WILSON, EDWIN. "Conflicting Elements in a Human Soul." Wall
    Street Journal, 28 October; New York Theatre Critics' Re-
    views, p. 203.
        Equus as a psychiatric detective story. One of the
    most powerful and provocative theatrical experiences of
    our time.


## 1975


1  ANON. "Brief on the Arts." New York Times, 4 June, p. 26.
       Outer Critics' Circle votes award to Peter Shaffer for
   Equus, its choice for the best play of the year.

2  BARNES, CLIVE. "Shaffer Drama Is Still Magnificent Theater."
   New York Times, 17 July, p. 19.
       Reports that Equus won every possible award for the
   season.

3  BUCKLEY, TOM. "'Write Me' Said the Play to Peter Shaffer."
   New York Times Magazine (13 April):20-21, 25-26, 28, 30,
   32, 34, 37-38, 40.
       Shaffer reveals details of the actual case that was the
   basis for Equus and talks about his play. Equus was controversial in part because of the long nude scene and in
   part because of the theme, which is a defense of insanity--
   the wellspring of artistic creativity. The final script
   was endorsed by an emminent London child psychiatrist.
   Quotes Shaffer as saying: "I do not believe that Art and
   insanity have anything to say to each other. The greatest
   Art--the symphonies of Haydn or the paintings of Bellini--
   virtually defines sanity for me."

4  CALTA, LOUIS. "Equus Voted Best Play by Drama Critics'
   Circle." New York Times, 28 May, p. 30.
       Award for Best Play of the 1974-1975 theater season.

5  DEFORD, FRANK. "Peter Shaffer's Equus Celebrates the Horse
   as an Awesome Pagan Idol." Sports Illustrated (3 March):
   9.
       Reservations about Equus as drama but not as theater,
   largely because of the horses. Horses as they relate to
   cowboys and jockeys is the central focus of the review.

1975

6  GREER, EDWARD G.  Review of Equus.  Drama 117 (Summer):32.
        Now that Equus is playing in a country "where Freud has
   for years been a household God," there has been a reaction
   against the methods used in the play and of Dysart's in-
   volvement with his patient.

7  GUERNSEY, OTIS L., ed.  The Best Plays of 1974-1975.  New
        York:  Dodd, Mead & Co., pp. 133-56.
        Includes an abridged version of Equus and a brief bio-
   graphical sketch of Shaffer.

8  HEWES, HENRY.  "The Crime of Dispassion."  Saturday Review
        (25 January):54.
        Equus is the most strikingly successful of the many
   British imports of the year.  The play's statement is "less
   impressive than is Shaffer's skillful theatrical fabrica-
   tion, which deftly finds layers of comic relief" as he
   drills into a rock of tragedy.  A surprisingly painless
   modern tragedy is the result.  At its truest when it is
   reflecting Shaffer's anger at his own civilization.

9  KERR, WALTER.  "Sherlock and Equus Revisited."  New York Times,
        5 October, sec. 2, pp. 1, 5.
        After seeing Equus for the second time during which he
   could no longer participate in the mystery, the critic
   starts to ask:  Is the play fair to psychiatry?  Is there
   a core of homosexuality between doctor and patient?  Are
   the eyes that Alan puts out the eyes of God, the only God
   he worships?

10  LERNER, MAX.  "The Best Plays."  New York Post, 9 May, p. 41.
        On Shaffer's Equus and Albee's Seascape, two "idea"
   plays that have won the recognition they deserve in the
   forms of popular and/or critical success.

11  LYNCH, WILLIAM F.  "What's Wrong with Equus?  Ask Euripides."
        America 133 (13 December):419-22.
        When contrasted with the great play Bacchae by
   Euripides, the master of passion, Equus emerges as a
   miserable act of imagination.  (Much of the article, in
   fact, is about Bacchae.)  Equus is beset by the limited
   view that passion, madness, and intuition are a better
   fate than sanity, reason, and ordinariness.  All of the
   images and rhythm of the play becloud the issue of why the
   audience is so captivated by it.  Equus is at once a magnificent and monstrous play.

12  NOVICK, JULIUS.  "Equus Rehorsed."  Village Voice, 1 September,

pp. 79-80.
The play remains perplexing, even with a new cast. It
is still vivid and memorable, but not emotionally involv-
ing. Almost, or perhaps too, perfect in design and execution. A "flamingly romantic" work proclaiming the value
of madness over sanity.

13 REAL, JERE. "A Rocking Horse Winner." National Review (31
January):114-15.
Rich complexities in Equus. Shaffer has successfully
and deeply explored the myth-making necessity of man.

14 REED, REX. "Perkins Improves Equus." New York Daily News,
14 November, p. 82.
With Anthony Perkins playing the role of Dysart, Equus
is really a "human" play.

15 RICHARDSON, JACK. "The English Invasion." Commentary (February):76-78.
Shaffer is a playwright of very modest talents who was
competent with Five Finger Exercise and the thin but
pleasant Black Comedy. When he attempted The Royal Hunt of
the Sun, he ended up with a public school history pageant
and made of a conflict in cultures an exercise in English
badinage. In Equus, a humble play pretends to discuss the
whole question of cultural vitality--the Apollonian and
Dionysian dichotomy.

16 SHAFFER, PETER. Comments on Equus. Vogue (February):136-37,
192.
Shaffer on Equus, Jung, and the theater, which has to
be "an ecstatic and alarming experience. And a beautiful
one."

17 SIMON, JOHN. "Hippodrama at the Psychodrome." Hudson Review
28 (Spring):97-106.
Purports to examine the success of Equus on Broadway,
but rather presents a severe criticism of the play and
attempts to prove that it is somehow a defense of homosexuality and a dishonest defense at that.

18 SONTAG, FREDERICK. "God's Eyes Everywhere." Christian Century (17 December):1162, 1164.
Equus is about God, and its theme is that God is always
watching us. But in Equus, He is a God of suffering and
of vengeance and not a God of redemption. Elaborately explains the Christian implications of the play's philosophy
[as the critic reads it] and concludes that Christianity

1975

can "weave a path of understanding through the darkness in which the psychiatrist stands at the end of the play."

19  TOBIAS, TOBI.  "Playing without Words."  Dance Magazine (May): 48–50.
     Primarily concerned with the role of the horse–actors in Equus.

20  VANDENBROUCKE, RUSSELL.  "Equus:  Modern Myth in the Making." Drama and Theatre 12:129–33.
     Its impressive title notwithstanding, the article is mostly plot summary.

21  WAKEMAN, JOHN, ed.  World Authors 1950–1970.  New York:  H. W. Wilson Co., pp. 1289–90.
     Biographical sketch and commentary on Shaffer's plays.

22  WEALES, GERALD.  "Horse Choler."  Commonweal (25 April):78–79.
     What polite audience could resist the combination of sex, religion, and violence?  But there is something too concocted about the mechanism, the transformation of therapy.

23  WEIGHTMAN, JOHN.  "Christ as Man and Horse."  Encounter (March):44–46.
     Equus, to some extent, is a good play.  "The real poetic interest in life lies in suffering, which we elimi- nate too easily on rationalistic grounds."  Sees this attitude as being of dubious merit; it keeps the play from being taken seriously as dramatic literature.  Hesther is never allowed to formulate any really cogent arguments to counter Dysart's (that is, Shaffer's) point of view. Dysart's nonsexual, nonlyrical marriage serves only as a contrast with Alan's modus vivendi; it is not necessary in the play, except to give the psychiatrist a chance for self-pity.  Who can be so sentimental as to cling to myth or religion or to muddled suffering, rather than lucid vision?

24  WEINER, BERNARD.  "Does Equus Need Sex and Violence."  San Francisco Chronicle, 26 February, p. 48.
     Shaffer is an accomplished playwright and is not using sex in order to break into the theater.  The nude horse- blinding scene "nearly takes on the power of Greek tragedy."

25  "Yeas and Nays for Equus."  New York Times, 5 January, sec. 2, p. 5.

*Peter Shaffer*

1976

Four letters to the editor in response to Sanford
Gifford's review of the play.  (See also Part I 1974.7.)


<u>1976</u>

1  ANON.  Blurb on <u>Equus</u> which appeared frequently.  <u>New Yorker</u>
   (<u>31 May</u>):4.
      "Peter Shaffer's continously exciting dance of explora-
   tion through the mind of a boy who loves horses, worships
   the quality of 'horseness,' and commits a dreadful crime in
   the name of that worship."  [One sentence, which sums up
   perfectly the letter and the spirit of the play.]

2  ANON.  "<u>Equus</u> Owners Plan Two Moves--One on Broadway, One for
   Road."  <u>New York Times</u>, 14 September, p. 45.
      Move planned to the Helen Hayes Theatre with Anthony
   Perkins in the role of Dysart.  A national tour is also
   planned.

3  ANON.  "Shaffer Double Bill at the Shaw."  <u>Times</u> (London),
   11 June, p. 9.
      Announces the opening of <u>Black Comedy</u> and <u>The White</u>
   <u>Liars</u>.  Paul Giovanni worked with Shaffer on the rewriting of <u>White Lies</u> and directed the two plays.

4  ANON.  Success of <u>Equus</u>.  <u>New York Times</u>, 9 July, p. C2.
      <u>Equus</u>, which recently opened in Los Angeles, will also
   play in Mexico City, Paris, and Vienna.

5  BOSWORTH, PATRICIA.  "Richard Burton:  'I Knew If I Didn't
   Come Back Now I Never Would.'"  <u>New York Times</u>, 4 April,
   sec. 2, pp. 5, 10.
      Burton on the character of Dysart--an eccentric, driven,
   isolated, and overworked man.

6  BURLAND, J. ALEXIS.  "Discussion of Papers on <u>Equus</u>."  <u>Inter-</u>
   <u>national Journal of Psychoanalytic Psychotherapy</u> 5:501-6.
      Concluding remarks on the papers presented at the
   Association for Applied Psychoanalysis; 13 June 1975.
   <u>Equus</u> is not a tragedy since if does not contain "noble
   intentions."  The play may not be judged on criteria and
   nomenclature established by the American Psychological
   Association because it is a play and not a situation of
   "free association."  [Dr. Burland is a medical child psychoanalyst.]

7  CUSHMAN, ROBERT.  "Better Black than White."  <u>Observer</u> (London),

1976

4 July, p. 22.
  Black Comedy is probably the only classic farce written
in England since World War Two.  It is a mechanical joke
that becomes irresistible.  The White Liars, "like many of
Shaffer's [plays, suffers] from its failure to find a believable idiom."

 *8  DENEULIN, ALAIN.  "Equus."  Kunst en Cultuur (Brussels), 1
     April, pp. 14-16.
       Listed in the MLA International Bibliography, 1976, p.
     139.

  9  ELSOM, JOHN.  Post-War British Theatre.  London, Henley-on-
     Thames, and Boston:  Routledge & Kegan Paul, pp. 96-98.
       Comments on Shaffer's major plays and compares the work
     with that of his contemporaries.

 10  GIFFORD, SANFORD.  "'Pop' Psychoanalysis, Kitsch, and the 'As
     If' Theater:  Further Notes on Peter Shaffer's Equus."
     International Journal of Psychoanalytic Psychotherapy 5:
     463-71.
       Text of a paper presented at the Association for Applied
     Psychoanalysis; 13 June 1975.  Examines Dr. Stamm's article
     and Dr. Glenn's work on Shaffer.  (See Part I 1974.9, 10,
     11; 1976.8 and 27.)  Futility of subjecting Equus to a
     "traditional psychoanalytic investigation, as a product of
     the playwright's unconscious, when the play represents a
     skillful, highly conscious use of analytic cliches to
     manipulate the audience."  Differences between Equus and
     "real" art and "real" tragedy, and why it does not deserve
     the "serious scrutiny" given to great works of art.  (See
     also Part I 1974.7.)

 11  GLENN, JULES.  "Alan Strang as an Adolescent:  A Discussion of
     Peter Shaffer's Equus."  International Journal of Psycho-
     analytic Psychotherapy 5:473-87.
       Text of a paper presented at the Association for Applied
     Psychoanalysis; 13 June 1975.  Using Alan as the basis of
     a study in psychotic, adolescent behavior, comments that
     during adolescence there is an attraction and antagonism
     toward one's parents.  Alan's attempt at sex with Jill re-
     sults in impotence as he is invaded by oedipal images and
     prohibitions.  Alan's fantasies of being fused with the
     horse resemble those of children who picture themselves
     fused with their mothers; Equus the horse became the god
     with which Alan could be united.  The attack on the horses'
     eyes was a displaced attack on the restrictive father, who
     was always watching him.  Concludes that Dysart never uses

64

real psychoanalysis, only hypnosis in order to produce a
catharsis.

12  GRANT, STEVE. Review of Equus. Plays and Players (June):29.
      Equus is now acknowledged as a minor masterpiece, but
    Shaffer has neither the "objective correlative" nor the
    "compensatory verbal power with which to prop up what is a
    fairly routine philosophy." The character of Dysart is
    also weak. A vastly overrated play and a dangerous one,
    too: "Laingian pseudo-liberal manure."

13  GUSSOW, MEL. "Burton Finds a New Stage to Conquer." New
    York Times, 27 February, p. 16.
      Mostly about Richard Burton, who comments on Dysart's
    character and on the relationship between the psychiatrist
    and Alan.

14  LEE, JAMES. "Equus, Round Three." Exchange 2 (Spring):49-59.
      Round One is the rave, opening-night reviews. Round
    Two is the later objection to the play. Round Three takes
    the criticism full circle. Writes against Gifford's
    attack (Round Two) on Equus. (See Part I 1974.7.) Through
    its dramatic expertise, Equus works as well as any play
    New York has seen in quite some time.

15  LEONARD, JOHN. "Critic's Notebook: An Evening with Two
    Walking Anachronisms." New York Times, 26 May, p. 24.
      "Equus is a not very good play, brilliantly staged."

16  MACDONALD, JOHN W., and SAXTON, JOHN C., eds. The Royal Hunt
    of the Sun. Introduction by A. W. England. London:
    Longman Group.
      Historical note, notes, and exercises for their sixth
    edition of Shaffer's play. Contains biographical sketch
    of the playwright and an analysis of the play's themes,
    characters, structure, and language.

17  NIGHTINGALE, BENEDICT. "Horse Sense." New Statesman (30
    April):583.
      Equus is too neatly put together and too easily untied.
    It is critical of psychiatry, while using its messages;
    the horse is too many symbols all at once. But the play
    has some good points, such as giving Mrs. Strang a speech
    of self-justification.

18  OPPENHEIMER, GEORGE. Review of Equus. Long Island Newsday,
    14 March, sec. 2, p. 9.
      Essentially on the new cast, but also calls Equus "one

1976

of the few important dramas of the past decade."

19   RICH, ALAN.  "Of Men and Other Beasts."  <u>New York</u> Magazine
        (15 March):75.
            The play is ruined by the part of Dysart and remains a
        "non event."

20   SÁNCHEZ ARNOSI, MILAGROS.  "Acerca de <u>Equus</u>, de Peter
        Schaffer."  <u>Arbor:  Revista gereral de investigación y
        cultura</u> 93 (March):121-24.
            Places Shaffer (whose name she mispells) in the genera-
        tion of Beckett and Ionesco.  States the obvious about
        <u>Equus</u> and regrets that Shaffer's work is not better known
        in Spain; blames that fact on the lack of a bibliography
        of his work in Spanish.

21   SCHULTZ, DIETER.  "Peter Shaffer:  <u>The Royal Hunt of the Sun</u>."
        In <u>Das englische Drama der Gegenwart:  Interpretationen</u>.
        Edited by Oppel Horst.  Berlin:  Erich Schmidt, pp. 107-
        19.
            Examines the play from the perspectives of history,
        characters, and staging, and Shaffer in comparison with
        such writers as Artaud, Brecht, and Melville.  Concludes
        that Shaffer does not convincingly portray either the
        problems of existentialism or that of the conquest of Peru,
        and that the combination of the elements of chronicle play,
        Theater of Cruelty, character tragedy, and idea play does
        not provide a synthesis but rather a conglomeration in
        which the individual parts cancel each other out and
        leave a vacuum, which Dexter's staging cannot hide.  In
        German.

22   SHAFFER, PETER.  "Peter Shaffer on Faith, Farce and Masks."
        <u>Listener</u> (14 October):476-77.
            Shaffer on religion in <u>Equus</u> and in real life and on
        the art of playwriting.

*23  SIMONS, PIET.  "K.V.S. op toernee met <u>Equus</u>."  <u>Ons Erfdeel:
        Algemeen-Nederlands Tweemaundelijks Kultureel Tijdschrift</u>
        (Rekkem) 19:449.  ("K.V.S. on a Journey with <u>Equus</u>."  <u>Our
        Heritage:  General Netherlands Bi-monthly Cultural Journal</u>.)
            Listed in the <u>MLA International Bibliography</u>, 1977,
        p. 129.

24   SLUTZKY, JACOB E.  "<u>Equus</u> and the Psychopathology of Passion."
        <u>International Journal of Psychoanalytic Psychotherapy</u>
        5:489-500.
            Text of a paper presented at the Association for Applied

Psychoanalysis; 13 June 1975.  Discusses Equus in terms of
its view of the concept of passion.  Both Alan and Dysart
suffer from a pathology of passion:  Alan in his psychotic
identification with horses; Dysart in his inhibition of
passion.  Concludes that Equus can be seen as "a deeply
moving artistic portrayal of very powerful resistence to
psychotherapy."  [Dr. Slutzky is a psychologist in private
practice.]

25  SPURLING, HILARY.  "Horse-Play in Hampshire."  Observer
    (London), 25 April, p. 26.
        Equus is, in large part, a "documentary case history on
    an unexacting level far removed from these majestic imagi-
    nary horses."  Stripped of the central puzzle of why Alan
    committed his crime, it is a "fairly standard soap opera."
    Comparison between the work of Shaffer and that of J. M.
    Barrie.

26  STACY, JAMES R.  "The Sun and the Horse:  Peter Shaffer's
    Search for Worship."  Educational Theatre Journal 28
    (October):325-35.
        Not Shaffer's, as the title suggests, but rather Alan
    Strang's and the fictional Pizarro's search for worship.
    In both The Royal Hunt of the Sun and Equus, Shaffer enters
    into the world of magic, ritual, primitivism, and reli-
    gious passion in search of worship.  Pizarro and Dysart
    are both without worship in a sterile, materialistic world.
    "The idea of multiplicity of gods is central to Shaffer's
    concept of worship.  To him, organized society, with its
    governments, industries, and churches, is necessarily re-
    strictive, and detrimentally so."  In both plays, conven-
    tional religions not only fail to provide adequate spiri-
    tual fulfillment, they also act negatively to defeat or
    distort the spirit of the primitives.  Shaffer's intention
    is to use sex as a passion with which the audience can
    readily identify and to seek an even more transcendent,
    intense, meaningful passion than in religion--the anthro-
    pological origins of which are linked with sex.  If
    Atahuallpa becomes a corpse, then Alan becomes a ghost.
    The Inca dies literally, the boy spiritually; neither is
    resurrected.  Neither Pizarro nor Dysart finds the meaning
    he is seeking, but in the search both glimpse the shadow
    of the soul.  Shaffer hopes to arouse the same doubts in
    the audience and send it away looking for new meanings.
    He discounts conventional religions and other bonds as
    detrimental because they lock one into predetermined,
    structural worship and lives that have no regard for the
    reality of self--the multiplicity of self, which demands

1976

a multiplicity of gods. The products of modern churches
are of two kinds: the conventional believer with the
wrong answers (Valverde, De Nizza, Mrs. Strang); and the
nonbeliever with no answers (Pizarro and Dysart). When
new answers arise from passionate, primitive worshipers
(Atahuallpa and Alan), the spirits of Shaffer's nonbeliev-
ers flare up with the hope that they have found an answer.
But the bond is too much for them and it destroys the
worshippers along with the hope. Shaffer had Dysart cure
Alan in order to have a final scene for act 2 to parallel
that of act 1. Pizarro kills Atahuallpa because Shaffer
had to make that concession to history.

27 STAMM, JULIAN L. "Peter Shaffer's Equus--A Psychoanalytic
   Exploration." International Journal of Psychoanalytic
   Psychotherapy 5:449-61.
       Text of a paper read at the Association for Applied
   Psychoanalysis; 13 June 1975. Interprets Dysart's dream
   as a microcosm of the play and elaborately and penetrat-
   ingly examines each element of it. Considers the fantasies
   of both the doctor and the patient and makes much of the
   oedipal suggestions. Discusses the relationship between
   Alan and Dysart. [Dr. Stamm is an analyst and a lecturer
   in psychiatry.]

28 WARDLE, IRVING. "What Comes after a Smash?" Times (London),
   29 June, p. 8.
       The White Liars looks like a play written to fill a
   gap; the rewriting from White Lies did not benefit the
   play. Black Comedy is as good as ever.

29 WETZSTEON, ROSS. "Burton's Equus: They Shoot Actors, Don't
   They?" Village Voice, 8 March, p. 92.
       Equus: "an intellectual sham [and] a loathsome, mere-
   tricious piece of patronizing claptrap."


                              1977

1 BARNET, SYLVAN; BERMAN, MORTON; and BURTO, WILLIAM. Types of
   Drama: Plays and Essays. 2d ed. Boston: Little, Brown
   & Co., pp. 250-99.
       Contains the text of Equus; a paragraph on Shaffer's
   life; and a study of the play which mentions Freud's
   "Little Hans" case and also brings in Sophocles's Oedipus
   Rex, Shakespeare's King Lear, and Melville's Moby Dick.
   The staging of Equus is that of a courtroom, with Alan as
   both the witness and the criminal at the bar.

2  CORBALLY, JOHN.  "The Equus Ethic."  New Laurel Review 7,
   no. 2:53-58.
       In Equus, Shaffer seems to be saying that beneath a
   veneer of social convention, "man is a raving lunatic
   beast" and he also seems "to applaud the fact."  Equus
   can be seen as advocating a wholesale tearing down of an
   ordered society, but offers no new model and seems to opt
   for chaos.  It knocks down everything that gives society
   coherence:  family, religion, intellect, therapy, and opts
   for anarchy; man may follow his favorite commandment re-
   gardless of the consequences.  The play is dangerous because "the reader is left with his own bare passions and
   perhaps a spike clutched in his hands."  Claims that Frank
   spends "all of his spare time" at pornographic movies and
   speculates that Alan was only "temporarily" impotent.

3  EDWARDS, BILL.  Award for Equus.  Variety, 6 April, p. 119.
       Shaffer wins the Los Angeles Drama Critics' Award.

4  GIANAKARIS, C. J.  "Theatre of the Mind in Miller, Osborne,
   and Shaffer."  Renascence 30 (Autumn):33-42.
       In Equus, Shaffer modifies both Naturalism and Expres-
   sionism into a stage tableau for a glimpse at a question-
   ing soul.  Dysart is a modern-day Hamlet in a courtroom-
   type situation, defending his conduct as though to a jury.

5  GOTTFRIED, MARTIN.  "Alec McCowen Stifles Equus."  New York
   Post, 24 February, p. 18.
       The play is an electrifying theatrical experience.

6  NASSO, CHRISTINE, ed.  Contemporary Authors:  A Bio-Biblio-
   graphical Guide to Current Authors and Their Work.  Rev.
   ed.  Vols. 25-28.  Detroit:  Gale Research Co., pp. 650-
   52.
       A chronology with criticism.

7  PALMER, HELEN H.  European Drama Criticism 1900-1975.  2d ed.
   Folkestone, England:  Shoe String Press, pp. 476-78.
       Contains a partial list of reviews of Five Finger Exer-
   cise, The Public Eye, The Private Ear, The Royal Hunt of
   the Sun, Black Comedy, White Lies, The White Liars, and
   Equus.

8  TERRIER, SAMUEL.  "Equus:  Human Conflicts and the Trinity."
   Christian Century (18 May):472-76.
       A Christian approach to Equus.  The appeal of Equus is
   that it compels audiences to ask themselves to question
   the ultimate meaning of life.  The hero of the play is

Equus, the image of God, as each person conceives of Him
in his own unconscious.  More than just sexual fulfill-
ment, Alan is looking for a mystical union with infinity;
like a medieval mystic who tries to lose himself within
Jesus, Alan rides Equus at midnight.  The midnight rides
are a sacramental means of identification with a Christ
who tramples his enemies.  The play is a quest for being
One Person and a study of the starvation for transcen-
dence.  Shaffer knows the problem, but not the cure.
Equus opens the public's eyes to the religious autoeroti-
cism of our age.  It prompts the audience to look again
at the mystery of the Christian faith through the analogy
of parental, filial, and professional conflicts.

9  VINSON, JAMES, ed.  Contemporary Dramatists.  2d ed.  London:
   St. James Press; New York:  St. Martin's Press, pp. 710-
   13.  [1st ed., 1973.]
      John Elsom contributed a short biographical sketch;
   complete list of Shaffer's plays, film, radio, and television scripts, and novels; penetrating and intelligent
   commentary on the plays.  Recognizes Shaffer as one of the
   few British dramatists to have achieved major public and
   critical success without ever belonging to a "school" or
   "movement."  Without being avant-garde or staunchly con-
   servative, Shaffer keeps an open mind, and as a result has
   written "perhaps the best modern farce, Black Comedy, one
   of the best epics, The Royal Hunt of the Sun, one of the
   best domestic dramas, Five Finger Exercise . . . and an
   ambitious philosophical drama, The Battle of Shrivings."
   Shaffer's dialogue may lack brilliance and may on occasion
   become too literary and sententious, but he knows how to
   tell a good story and has the capacity to use whatever
   dramatic means that seem appropriate.  His plays are held
   together by strong basic conflicts--cultural, emotional,
   or social.  There is an underlying humanism which over-
   rides the hatred in the plots.  Shaffer is an optimistic
   writer, an instinctive humanist, whose plays usually end
   with a firm statement of the importance of love and understanding.
      Incorrectly calls "The Merry Roosters' Panto" "It's
   about Cinderella," which, according to Shaffer, was never
   the title of the piece; mistakenly classifies The Woman in
   the Wardrobe, Shaffer's 1951 novel, as having been written
   jointly by both Peter and Anthony Shaffer. [Shaffer said
   that he wrote that novel alone.]

*Peter Shaffer*

## 1978

1 DEAN, JOAN F. "Peter Shaffer's Recurrent Character Type." <u>Modern Drama</u> 21, no. 3:297-305.
   <u>The Royal Hunt of the Sun</u>, <u>Shrivings</u>, and <u>Equus</u> are complementary pieces, shedding light on one another and on middle-aged men in crises of faith. Pizarro, Mark Askelon, and Dysart all experience profound dissatisfaction with their cultures and existences, and their crises are exacerbated through contact with primitive cultures. Modern society fails to provide a constructive vehicle for man's religious impulses.

*2 KŁOSSOWICZ, JAN; KOENIG, JERZY; SITO, JERZY S.; and WYSIŃKA, ELŻBIETA. "<u>Equus</u>: czyli mechanizm sukcesu." <u>Dialog: Miesięcznik Poświęcony Dramaturgii Współczesnej: Teatralnej, Filmowej, Radiowej, Telewizyjnej</u> (Warsaw) 23, no. 8: 146-52. ("<u>Equus</u> or the Mechanism of Success." <u>Dialogue: Monthly Devoted to Contemporary Dramaturgy: Theater, Film, Radio, Television.</u>)
   Listed in the <u>MLA International Bibliography</u>, 1978, 155. [On <u>Equus</u> and its publication in Poland.]

3 LOUNSBERRY, BARBARA. "'God-Hunting': The Chaos of Worship in Peter Shaffer's <u>Equus</u> and <u>Royal Hunt of the Sun</u>." <u>Modern Drama</u> 21, no. 1:13-28.
   An anthropological approach to Shaffer's two masterpieces, each of which is "an exploration of man's search for gods, and how they ultimately elude them." God-hunting supplies the structure of both plays; the multiplicity of gods is the source of dramatic conflict; the central god images supply the intellectual and emotional power of the plays. De Soto and Hesther encourage the god-hunters, supply the ethical and moral impetus for the hunts, and provide an unchallenged symbol of the status quo. Alan's Equus is made up of conflicting aspects of the gods of his society, and Shaffer is suggesting that Alan's pathology is really society's pathology, due to the inability to establish a hierarchy of priorities among the conflicting gods. Shaffer recognizes the need for gods and for worship, but also that such idealism is incompatible with reality. Evidence to support a relationship between the two plays is supplied by a reproduction of a Celtic candelabra and from a tarot card.

*Peter Shaffer*

1979

## 1979

1  APPLE, R. W., Jr. "Portrait of Mozart As a Loudmouth." <u>New
   York Times</u>, 11 November, sec. 2, p. 8.
      <u>Amadeus</u> is the "theatrical event of the season."
   Shaffer has been haunted by the "extinction of divinity,"
   and in <u>Amadeus</u> he shows "the god of music dying in his
   slum, watched by the worshipper who has destroyed him."
   Mozart is depicted as vain, coarse, and loudmouthed; shown
   entirely through the eyes of Salieri, who may have poisoned
   him.  Received more attention than might otherwise have
   been the case because of a shortage of good British plays
   this season.

2  BARBER, JOHN. "Mozart Depicted as a Popinjay." <u>Daily Tele-
   graph</u> (London), 5 November, p. 15.
      Review of <u>Amadeus</u>. The play uses too many words to
   describe the perils of genius and the complexity of the
   men it possesses, but some of the scenes are brilliant.

3  BERMAN, JEFFREY. "<u>Equus</u>: 'After Such Little Forgiveness
   What Knowledge?'" <u>Psychoanalytic Review</u> 66, no. 3:
   407-22.
      A psychoanalytic approach that considers such matters
   as the Oedipus complex, castration fear, infantile sexuality, guilt and repression, and resistence and transfer-
   ence.  Speculates on a Shaffer-Dysart identification. [The
   critic is an English professor and not a professional
   psychoanalyst.]

4  BILLINGTON, MICHAEL. "Divining for a Theme." <u>Manchester
   Guardian</u>, 5 November, p. 11.
      "Big, bold, extravagantly theatrical play."  Two male pro-
   tagonists locked in combat:  one represents will and
   energy; the other is touched with the divine and finally
   crushed.  Form of a death bed confession by Salieri, court
   composer to Emperor Joseph II.  First half better than
   second half, in which the characters represent god and god-
   destroyer.  Metaphysical confrontation between Envious
   Mediocrity and Harassed God.  The writing goes from tight
   and precise to extremely flatulent.  "Shaffer has lit upon
   a fascinating human drama but finally tried to wrench it
   to fit his recurrent theme of the destruction of divinity."

5  ESSLIN, MARTIN.  Review of <u>Amadeus</u>.  <u>Plays and Players</u>
   (November):20-21, 27-28.
      Themes:  the mysteries of the genius of the creative
   process, the contrast between the overcivilized and the

natural man, sexual restraint and the free flow of self-
expression through sex. Man of modest talent consumed by
envy of one of the world's greatest natural geniuses.
Striking parallels between this play and Pushkin's <u>Mozart
and Salieri</u> (1832). Complexly built on an epic scale, and
that is the problem--neither the language nor the form is
up to the subject matter. The tragedy is Salieri's: "It
is just not fair!" And he turns against God, to Whom he
had prayed for talent and fame. Mozart emerges as a figure
of grotesque inappropriateness. Salieri devotes himself
to Mozart's destruction by playing on his fears. The
language is flat. Two pages of photographs of the London
production.

6  FENTON, JAMES. Blurb on <u>Amadeus</u>. <u>Sunday Times</u> (London), 18
   November, p. 38.
      Blurb which appeared weekly: "Appalling new play by
   author of <u>Equus</u>, plasticated production by Peter Hall.
   Paul Scofield mediocre as Salieri, Simon Callow and
   Felicity Kendal do their best as the Mozarts." (See fol-
   lowing item.)

7  _____. "Can We Worship This Mozart?" <u>Sunday Times</u> (London),
   23 December, p. 43.
      What purports to be a drama review results as an attack
   on Shaffer. The intent is to show that <u>Amadeus</u> is in poor
   taste. The play is "perfectly nauseating"; appalling is
   too generous a word for it. Mozart is depicted with
   "dreadful and offensive banality," because he is seen
   through the eyes of a very, very bad dramatist--perhaps
   the worst serious English playwright since John Drinkwater.

8  GOODWIN, JOHN. Letter to the <u>Sunday Times</u> (London), 30 December, p. 10.
      Responds to Fenton's review of <u>Amadeus</u> of the previous
   week. Fenton's attack only proves that <u>Amadeus</u> is a work
   of "rare power." [Mr. Goodwin is the head of the National
   Theatre Press Office.] (See previous item.)

9  GOW, GORDON. "The Struggle: An Interview with John Dexter."
   <u>Plays and Players</u> (November):14-16.
      On Dexter's career, part of which included directing
   <u>Black Comedy</u>, <u>The Royal Hunt of the Sun</u>, and <u>Equus</u>. Includes a photograph of a scene from <u>The Royal Hunt of the
   Sun</u>.

10  GRANT, STEVE. "Much Ado about Mozart." <u>Observer</u> (London),
    11 November, p. 16.

1979

Shaffer's treatment of the Mozart-Salieri legend is
"slavishly authentic" in its details, but "grossly un-
historical." Shaffer, who passes for a man of ideas, is a
master of suspension of disbelief. The play creaks with
the mechanics of drama, is often silly and self-indulgent,
and occasionally overblown with empty rhetoric: pure
Shaffer. It is, however, a feast for the ears.

11 HAMILTON, JAMES W. "Equus and the Creative Process." Journal
of the Philadelphia Association for Psychoanalysis 6:53-64.
Proposes "to approach Equus as a function of the playwright's need to master certain conflicts pertaining to
twinship, and to understand more precisely specific com-
ponents of the creative process." Speculates on the relationship of the details in Shaffer's personal life and the
creation of Equus. Opines that "a central genetic deter-
minant in both Equus and The Royal Hunt of the Sun is that
of unresolved orality focused on questions of nurturance,
abandonment, basic trust, and separation-individuation
within the context of a twinship, the rage secondary to
deprivation and frustration being expressed primarily
through the characterizations of Pizarro and Alan Strang."
In addition, Shaffer attempts to "externalize his intrapsychic dilemmas allowing him to remobilize or evoke the
mythopoetic elements that were so striking in The Royal
Hunt of the Sun but not in The Battle of Shrivings." Concludes that: "By comparing Equus with The Royal Hunt of
the Sun, plays written by the same author, a continuance
of preoedipal themes is demonstrated, principally oral in
nature and highlighted by the quest for union with the
early, nurturing mother. The creative art, relying upon
mythopoesis as an important vehicle, is regarded as primarily a reparative gesture in the service of ego mastery
of intrapsychic conflict generated by the sibling rivalry
and the ambiguity over self and object representations
existing amongst twins, accentuated by the trauma of object loss." [Dr. Hamilton is Director of Psychiatry at
the Veterans Administration Medical Center in Wood, Wisconsin.]

12 JENSEN, GREGORY. "New London Play about Mozart's 'Murder.'"
San Francisco Examiner, 19 February, p. 31.
Salieri uses Machiavellian and petty ploys, as well as
the direct haunting of Mozart in order to drive him to an
early grave and thereby frustrate God, Who gave Mozart his
musical genius. If Salieri cannot go down in history for
his music, then he wanted his fame to come from having
murdered Mozart. "Shaffer seems to be standing up for the

mediocrities of this world" in his "overlong, intricate play."

13  KLEIN, DENNIS A. Peter Shaffer. Twayne English Author
    Series, no. 261. Boston: Twayne Publishers, 163 pp.
       The only full-length, published study of Shaffer's work.
    Examines in close detail all of the plays from Five Finger
    Exercise through Equus, as well as the early novels and
    scripts for radio and television, some of which are avail-
    able only at BBC headquarters or in Mr. Shaffer's personal
    collection. Traces development of themes, characters, and
    techniques. Much comparative material. Includes a
    chronology, biographical sketch, and bibliography.

14  NIGHTINGALE, BENEDICT. "In London, the Talk Is of Amadeus."
    New York Times, 23 December, sec. 2, pp. 5, 15.
       A résumé of the reviews of London's critics and a con-
    cluding question: "Does Mr. Shaffer's play deserve" Mr.
    Scofield's and Peter Hall's considerable talents?

15  _____. "Obscene Child." New Statesman (9 November):735.
       Amadeus adds little stature to Shaffer's reputation as
    a dramatist.

16  OTTEN, ALLEN L. "Arts Letter from London." Wall Street
    Journal, 21 December, p. 13.
       Amadeus is the most controversial play of the season.
    Exploration of the struggle between man and divinity.
    Strong audience enforcement: sold out for the entire
    month.

17  PIT. Review of Amadeus. Variety, 14 November, pp. 90, 92.
       "History as outlandish speculation." "A clever, pro-
    vocative and playful 'stunt.'" Broadway rights are held
    by the Shubert Organization.

18  POYSER, L. Letter to the Sunday Times (London), 30 December,
    p. 10.
       Counters Fenton's review of Amadeus (see Part I 1979.7)
    and calls the play "one of the best theatre productions
    for many a year," the foul language notwithstanding.

19  SHAFFER, PETER. "Figure of Death." Observer (London), 4
    November, p. 37.
       Shaffer on three mental pictures that inspired three
    plays: The Incas in a nighttime vigil, awaiting the
    resurrection of their sun god; a young man stabbing wildly
    at the eyes of a stableful of horses; Mozart surrounded by

a spectral haunter, the haunter's assistant, and Mozart's wife. The story of Amadeus was inspired by a legend that an ominous, unnamed figure came to Mozart and requested that he compose a Requiem Mass. Mozart, in his failing state, came to believe that God was the patron, and the Mass was for himself.

20 SUZY. "Wolfgang Scores Again in London." New York Daily News, 20 November, p. 12.
   Amadeus is the biggest hit the National Theatre has had and the play deserves all of its success.

21 Who's Who 1979-1980: An Annual Biographical Dictionary. New York: St. Martin's Press, pp. 2262-63.
   A list of Shaffer's plays and the theaters at which they opened in London and in New York.

22 WITMAN, BARRY B. "The Anger in Equus." Modern Drama 22, no. 1:61-66.
   Attempts to find parallels between Equus and Look Back in Anger. Concludes that: "In its world view, then, Equus is an extension not only of Look Back in Anger, but also of John Arden's Live Like Pigs, Arnold Wesker's Roots, Harold Pinter's The Loner, and numerous other dramatic ventures, which contrasted the passion of the abnormal with the drabness of the postwar English world, and which, consequently, have led to an often misplaced admiration of violence and aberration"; and that "what is ultimately applauded in Equus is not its message but its packaging. Like spectators of Marat-Sade, audiences at Shaffer's play are frequently carried headlong into a vague kind of catharsis without a very clear knowledge of what they are experiencing or applauding." Finds Equus ultimately to be "a schizophrenic play," whose theatrical fireworks cannot mask its "muddled logic" and "tired philosophy."

23 YOUNG, B. A. Review of Amadeus. Financial Times (London), 5 November, p. 15.
   No life in the story; unimaginative and as "hollow as a strip-cartoon."

## 1980

1 ANON. "Amadeus Is Best Play . . ." Variety, 30 January, p. 89.
   Named Best Play of 1979 by the London Evening Standard. Will open in New York next season.

1980

2  ANON. Blurb on <u>Amadeus</u>. <u>New Yorker</u> (29 December):2.
     "A highly intelligent Peter Shaffer thriller having to
   do, on one level, with the possibility that Mozart's early
   death was a result of his having been poisoned by a rival
   and, on another level, with that rival's indignant repu-
   diation of God."

3  BARNES, CLIVE. "<u>Amadeus</u>: A Total Triumph." <u>New York Post</u>,
   18 December, p. 39.
     Shaffer's best play to date. "A total, iridescent
   triumph." Far superior to Shaffer's text for the London
   production. A play to savor.

4  _____. "Change Aids <u>Amadeus</u>." <u>New York Post</u>, 31 December,
   p. 17.
     In London, <u>Amadeus</u> seemed as near to a masterpiece as
   Shaffer could ever write. After seeing the New York production, the critic withdraws any reservations that he had
   had about the play; minor and major changes have tightened
   the play with "sublime subtlety." More direct and dramatic
   than <u>Equus</u> in the presentation of its theme.

5  BEAUFORT, JOHN. "Mozart Murdered? Unlikely, but It Makes
   for an Unusual Play." <u>Christian Science Monitor</u>, 22
   December, p. 19.
     "Complex, darkly probing, richly theatrical. . . ."

6  FEINGOLD, MICHAEL. "Eine Kleine Nicht Musik." <u>Village Voice</u>,
   24-30 December, pp. 82-83.
     A review of <u>Amadeus</u> which accuses Shaffer of being the
   real mediocrity and which concludes that "if you prefer
   mediocrity to Mozart, <u>Amadeus</u> is definitely your dish."

7  GEIST, KENNETH L. "Was Mozart Murdered?" <u>After Dark</u> (October):32-33.
     Notes the "striking likenesses" that <u>Amadeus</u> bears to
   <u>Equus</u> as well as its similarity to <u>The Royal Hunt of the
   Sun</u> and to <u>Five Finger Exercise</u>. The play raises more
   issues than it answers, and Salieri's contradictory remarks that he did/did not poison Mozart are "as preposterous as they are confusing." But if <u>Amadeus</u> is "unpersua-
   sive as biography . . . it is full of theatrical pleasures."

8  GELATT, RONALD. "Peter Shaffer's <u>Amadeus</u>: A Controversial
   Hit." <u>Saturday Review</u> (November):11-14.
     Notes on Shaffer's life and work, as well as on his
   background in music. <u>Amadeus</u> has been a sellout at the
   National Theatre since the day it opened. Shaffer's re-

1980

search for <u>Amadeus</u> was done "fastidiously well." However unpleasant Mozart may seem, his depiction in <u>Amadeus</u> is true to fact. "<u>Amadeus</u> gives heartening evidence that there is still room for the play of ideas." Challenging and enthralling theme: "the eternal mystery of genius-- and the anguish many of us suffer recognizing how far short of genius our best efforts fall." French and German productions are planned, and there is talk of a film version.

9  GILL, BRENDAN. "Bargaining with God." <u>New Yorker</u> (29 December):54.
    A clever play by a clever man, who invites us to enter into the mind of Salieri.

10  HOBE. Review of <u>Amadeus</u>. <u>Variety</u>, 24 December, p. 62.
    Shaffer's writing has his "customary skill, tautness and dramatic compulsion." Artfully written. Strong bet for a film adaptation.

11  HUMMLER, RICHARD. "<u>Amadeus</u> Is New Installment in N. Y. Times Preview Serial." <u>Variety</u>, 24 December, pp. 63, 66.
    Against the desires of <u>Amadeus</u>'s management, Frank Rich attended and reviewed a preview performance rather than the opening night performance. (His review of the play was favorable. See 1980.23.)

12  KALEM, T. E. "Blood Feud." <u>Time</u> (29 December):57.
    The eternal triangle in <u>Amadeus</u>: two men pitted against each other under God's hateful or indifferent eyes. Shades of <u>The Royal Hunt of the Sun</u> and <u>Equus</u>.

13  KENYON, NICHOLAS. "More on the Don." <u>New Yorker</u> (24 March): 122.
    Not on Shaffer's work per se, but quotes him and makes reference to <u>Amadeus</u>, "a brilliantly diverting inquiry into the nature of genius."

14  KERNER, LEIGHTON. "Who Is This Salieri Guy and Why Are We Talking about Him?" <u>Village Voice</u>, 24–30 December, p. 81.
    Background information on Antonio Salieri and brief comments on <u>Amadeus</u>, "Shaffer's marvelous play."

15  KLEIN, DENNIS A. "Literary Onomastics in Peter Shaffer's <u>Shrivings</u> and <u>Equus</u>." <u>Literary Onomastic Studies</u> 7:127-38.
    On name symbolism in <u>Shrivings</u> and <u>Equus</u> and on how the names reveal the characters of the Strang family, Martin Dysart, and Hesther Salomon in <u>Equus</u>; and of Mark and David

Askelon and Gideon Petrie in Shrivings. Brief references
to The Woman in the Wardrobe, White Lies, and The White
Liars.

16  KROLL, JACK. "Mozart and His Nemesis." Newsweek (29 December):58.
     Peter Shaffer has mastered the art of writing the
Shaffer play--"a large-scale, large-voiced treatment of
large themes, whose essential superficiality is marked by
skillful theatricality. . . ." Amadeus is "a brilliant
surrogate for 'great' theater."

17  LAWSON, CAROL. "McKellen Sought to Star in Amadeus." New
York Times, 2 April, p. C21.
     Amadeus is scheduled to open in New York in November.
Peter Hall will direct, and Ian McKellan will probably
star.

18  MINER, MICHAEL D. "Grotesque Drama in the '70s." Kansas
Quarterly 14 (Fall):99-109.
     Includes Equus as one of its examples.

19  MORLEY, SHERIDAN. "Who Killed Mozart?" Playbill (November):
6, 9-10.
     Biographical information on Shaffer, comments on the
relationship between Amadeus and The Royal Hunt of the Sun
and Equus, and quotations by Shaffer on his new play: "At
the heart of Amadeus is the relationship between talent
and genius, and that between morality and art." Morley
comments that "Amadeus towers above other new plays of its
time in much the same way that Equus and Royal Hunt of the
Sun once did; all three are highly charged dramatic events
concerned with the struggle between Man and God, between
the mediocre and the divine, and all three are about an
ultimately futile attempt to deny or destroy the arbitrary
power of heaven. . . . Two-man conflicts have, of course,
always been at the heart of Shaffer's best writing. . . ."
Calls Shaffer one of the half-dozen most distinguished
playwrights of our time.

20  NOVICK, JULIUS. "Mozart and Shaffer's Craft." Village Voice,
24-30 December, p. 82.
     Shaffer keeps writing the same play, and it never fails
to be fascinating. The Royal Hunt of the Sun, Equus, and
Amadeus are all about "an older man, alienated and bitter,
who is obsessed with envy for a younger man's closer con-
nection to godhead; the older man becomes in some sense a
father-figure to the younger, and in some sense destroys

him."  Likely to be the season's "snob hit."

21  PANTER-DOWNES, MOLLIE.  "Letter from London."  New Yorker
      (10 March):138-40.
        Despite the rise in theater tickets in London and the
      difficulties that other plays are having, Amadeus is al-
      ways sold out.  The bitter Salieri feels that his life has
      been poisoned by a terrible trick perpetrated on him by
      God.  The theme of the play is Salieri's losing duel with
      God for the genius that Mozart received.

22  PLUNKA, GENE A.  "The Existential Ritual:  Peter Shaffer's
      Equus."  Kansas Quarterly 12 (Fall):87-97.
        Treats Equus in the context of Shaffer's dramatic
      creations, with the focus primarily on the roles of Alan
      and Dysart.  The existential search for identity is a
      major concern in all of Shaffer's plays.  Equus's popular-
      ity is due to its being a "spokesman" for the seventies,
      during which people were turning inward and trying to find
      themselves.  As such, Alan is the perfect antihero; he is
      a unique personality surrounded by role-players and
      phonies; he never conforms to his environment.

23  RICH, FRANK.  Review of Amadeus.  New York Times, 18 December,
      p. C17.
        A favorable review.  (See 1980.11.)

24  ROBERTSON, NAN.  "When a Top British Actor Faces a Top
      Director, Electricity Crackles."  New York Times, 5 Novem-
      ber, p. C25.
        Essentially on conflicts between director Sir Peter
      Hall and actor Ian McKellen.  Shaffer comments that he
      became interested in the Mozart-Salieri story as an "idle
      project in idle curiosity."  His play, he says, is about
      "the envy of genius by mediocrity and the relevance of
      human goodness to art."  Shaffer does not see Mozart as
      "coarse or scatological" but rather as "jolly" and "more
      outspoken than the letters of his day."  The real mystery
      of Mozart is his "ordinariness."

25  ROSENWALD, PETER J.  "Amadeus:  Who Murdered Mozart?"
      Horizon (February):33.
        Marvellous theater, probably the best play in London
      this season.  Perfect in every detail and spellbinding at
      every moment--even when the production seems better than
      the play itself.  Shaffer lets the audience decide whether
      or not Salieri actually did murder Mozart, and thereby
      keeps the audience intensely involved.  "A must for anyone

going to London. . . . A trans-Atlantic telephone call [to reserve tickets] is well worth the cost of the call."

26  SCHONBERG, HAROLD. "Mozart as 'A Silly Little Man.'" New York Times, 2 March, sec. 2, pp. 21, 27.
    The music critic praises Shaffer for having done "his homework" before writing Amadeus. Shaffer, who appears to have read everything written about Mozart, says that except for a few dramatic liberties, he tried to be "scrupulously accurate."

27  _____. "Mozart's World: From London to Broadway." New York Times, 14 December, sec. 2, pp. 1, 35.
    Warns of the portrait of Mozart that Shaffer depicts in the soon-to-open Amadeus. Shaffer stresses that he has written a play and not a biography--probable events, but not all historical. He conceived of Amadeus as an opera: the whispers of the populace as an opening chorus, the Venticelli as a duet, Salieri's speeches as arias.

28  SHAFFER, PETER. "Scripts in Trans-Atlantic Crossings May Suffer Two Kinds of Changes." Dramatists Guild Quarterly (Spring):29-33.
    Text of a discussion led by Shaffer at the Guild on changes that he has made in his plays so that they would be acceptable to American audiences; also on the differences between British and American audiences, and the mental changes that the audiences make in the plays. For example, Five Finger Exercise was somewhat outrageous for English audiences, but praised by Americans for its restraint and good manner; Shaffer had to take an incident out of act 2 of The Royal Hunt of the Sun and put it into act 1 (a change he regrets having made) because New York audiences do not like a longer second act than a first act; Equus was shocking in England for seeming cruel to animals, but in the United States for seeming cruel to psychiatrists. (Far more Americans than Britons are in analysis and loved hearing the psychological profession ridiculed.)

29  SIMON, JOHN. "'Amadequus,' or Shaffer Rides Again." New York Magazine (29 December/5 January 1981):62-63.
    Like Equus, another "middlebrow masterpiece."

30  WALLACH, ALLAN. "Peter Shaffer's Portrait of Mozart." Long Island Newsday, 18 December, pt. 2, p. 48.
    "A meditation on the nature of genius and the capriciousness of God." A vividly theatrical play. Shaffer

1980

weakens his case by overstating it.  The play approaches
grandeur when we hear Mozart's music and see Salieri's
reaction to it.

31  WATT, DOUGLAS.  "Amadeus Questions the Gift of Genius."  New
       York Daily News, 18 December, p. 63.
       A begrudgingly favorable review of the play.

32  WILSON, EDWIN.  "Peter Shaffer's Astigmatic View of God."
       Wall Street Journal, 19 December, p. 25.
       Scene after scene of highly charged drama.  Shaffer may
    raise more issues than he answers in Amadeus, but he "pro-
    vides the most ingenious and engrossing theater piece we
    have seen in some time."

# PART II
# ANTHONY SHAFFER

# Chronology

1952    How Doth the Little Crocodile? (with Peter Shaffer) published in Great Britain under the pseudonym Peter Antony.

1955    Withered Murder (novel; with Peter Shaffer) published in Great Britain.

1956    Withered Murder published in the United States.

1957    How Doth the Little Crocodile? (novel; with Peter Shaffer) published in the United States.

1963    "The Savage Parade" performed by the Repertory Players at the Globe Theatre in London on March 17.

1970    Sleuth opened at St. Martin's Theatre in London on February 12; at the Music Box in New York on November 12.

1975    Murderer opened at the Garrick Theatre in London on March 12.

1979    "The Case of the Oily Levantine" opened at Her Majesty's Theatre in London on September 13.

# Writings about Anthony Shaffer

## 1956

1   BOUCHER, ANTHONY. Review of <u>Withered Murder</u>. <u>New York Times</u>,
11 March, pp. 26–27.
See Part I 1956.1.


## 1957

1   BOUCHER, ANTHONY. Review of <u>How Doth the Little Crocodile?</u>
<u>New York Times</u>, 3 March, p. 31.
See Part I 1957.1.


## 1963

1   ANON. "Does Execution End Murder?" <u>Times</u> (London), 18
March, p. 7.
Notice of the performance of the previous day of "The
Savage Parade," about a secret trial in Israel of a former
S.S. officer and mass murderer of Jews.


## 1970

1   ANON. Review of <u>Sleuth</u>. <u>Time</u> (30 March):77.
Anthony Shaffer may have constructed a classic model in
<u>Sleuth</u> by satirizing all that he is doing in the play.

2   ANON. Review of <u>Sleuth</u>. WRVR-FM (New York) (12 November).
"Audiences get their money's worth of surprises, thrills
and shocks."

3   ANON. "Sleuthing." <u>Women's Wear Daily</u>, 22 October, pp. 4–5.
Anthony Shaffer on <u>Sleuth</u> and on his own history of
writing.

4   ANON.  "Who's Afraid of Stephen Sondheim?"  Variety, 25
      November, p. 49.
          Anthony Shaffer originally titled his play "Who's
      Afraid of Stephen Sondheim?" as a joke on his composer
      friend.  Sondheim objected, and Shaffer changed the title
      first to "Anyone for Tennis?" then to "Anyone for Murder?"
      and finally to Sleuth.

5   BARBER, JOHN.  Review of Sleuth.  Daily Telegraph (London),
      13 February, p. 16.
          It is all nonsense, but ingenious and too clever by
      half.

6   BARKER, FELIX.  Review of Sleuth.  Evening News (London),
      13 February, p. 6.
          The most ingenious detective play in years.

7   BARNES, CLIVE.  "Shaffer's Sleuth:  A Tale of Murder Opens
      at the Music Box."  New York Times, 13 November, p. 25;
      New York Theatre Critics' Reviews, p. 157.
          "It is good, neat, clean, and bloody fun . . . one of
      the most purely entertaining plays in many a season--an
      entrancing tale of detective-story mayhem with a touch of
      urbane intellectualism added for savor."  Characters play
      with urbane put-downs, civilized grace, and verbal daggers.
      Delicious writing of ponderous frivolity.  "A super show--
      the best of its genre since Dial M for Murder, and much
      cleverer."

8   BEAUFORT, JOHN.  "Tantalizing Game."  Christian Science Moni-
      tor, 20 November, p. 6.
          In the course of the battle of wits and wills, Shaffer
      takes swipes at British xenophobia, upper-class snobbery,
      racism, and a faulty educational system.

9   BILLINGTON, MICHAEL.  Review of Sleuth.  Plays and Players
      (April):34-35.
          "Sleuth is easily the most intelligent and compelling
      stage thriller since Dial M For [sic] Murder."  Sophisti-
      cated complexity and witty dialogue; an able parody of the
      very conventions the author is using:  "Rather like having
      Agatha Christie--written by John Mortimer."

10  BRYDEN, RONALD.  "Springboard for Dazzle."  Observer (London),
      15 February, p. 27.
          As brilliant a farce as Black Comedy, in its own way.
      Enjoyable even though it is contrived, involuted, and im-
      probable.

11  CHAPMAN, JOHN. "Sleuth--Rate It M for Murder and Mystery."
New York Daily News, 13 November; New York Theatre Critics'
Reviews, p. 157.
"One of the best melodramas I have ever seen. Maybe it
is the best. . . . Literate, witty, scary and filled with
sudden twists and tricks."

12  GILL, BRENDAN. Review of Sleuth. New Yorker (21 November):
103-4.
The subject is game-playing, as much among the characters as between author and audience. A wise investment.

13  GOLDMAN, DAVID. Review of Sleuth. CBS-Radio [13 November].
"The play is always intriguing, always suspenseful and
always well done. . . . The story is a beauty."

14  GOTTFRIED, MARTIN. Review of Sleuth. Women's Wear Daily,
13 November; New York Theatre Critics' Reviews, p. 158.
"Sleuth is a dumb play . . . because it claims to be
clever (and isn't) and spends all its time setting up
rules for games to play. . . ." A mystery and a parody of
one that is illogical from the start. "All feint and no
action," but intermittently interesting. Crudely devised
and uncertainly written.

15  GUSSOW, MEL. "With Sleuth Another Shaffer Catches Public
Eye." New York Times, 18 November, p. 38.
Anthony Shaffer gives background information on Sleuth
and mentions that his next play will be "Play with a
Gypsy," a psychological thriller.

16  HARRIS, LEONARD. Review of Sleuth. WCBS-TV (12 November);
New York Theatre Critics' Reviews, p. 160.
"Sleuth is a beauty . . . magnificently written."
Highly recommended fun. For "pure tingling entertainment,"
there is nothing better than Sleuth.

17  HEWES, HENRY. "Two Can Play at a Game." Saturday Review
(28 November):6.
The play suggests that there is a lethal danger in
mixing rational game-playing and irrational life-living.
The plot is a hokum of manufactured suspense and macabre
satire.

18  HIPP, EDWARD SOTHERN. "Sleuth, From London." Newark Evening
News, 13 November, p. 50.
An exercise in trickery that lives up to all of its ad-
vance publicity.

1970

19 _____. "The Thinking Man's Mystery." <u>Newark Sunday News</u>,
22 November, sec. 6, p. E4.
Absorbingly bizarre drama, abounding in skillful twists.
The dialogue is eerie as well as literate.

20 HOBE. Review of <u>Sleuth</u>. <u>Variety</u>, 18 November, p. 78.
An enthralling, amusing, baffling, and thoroughly satisfying mystery melodrama.

21 HOBSON, HAROLD. "And Now Anthony Shaffer." <u>Christian Science
Monitor</u>, 20 February.
Praises the play and the performances.

22 No Entry.

23 _____. Review of <u>Sleuth</u>. <u>Christian Science Monitor</u>, 20
June, p. 4.
The most accomplished mystery play that London has seen
since <u>Dial M for Murder</u>.

24 _____. "Shots in the Dark." <u>Sunday Times</u> (London), 15 February, p. 53.
"An outstanding example of the thriller considered as a
fine art . . ." and more brilliantly written than <u>Dial M
for Murder</u>.

25 HOPE-WALLACE, PHILIP. Review of <u>Sleuth</u>. <u>Manchester Guardian</u>,
13 February, p. 8.
Most ingenious.

26 KALEM, T. E. Review of <u>Sleuth</u>. <u>Time</u> (23 November):100.
Anthony Shaffer has written "a flawless murder mystery
. . . urbanely clever, unashamedly literate, clawingly
tense and playfully savage." If not the best of its genre,
certainly neck and neck with whichever is: consummate
spoof of thrillers.

27 KERR, WALTER. "Suave Grand Guignol." <u>New York Times</u>, 22
November, sec. 2, p. 18; <u>New York Theatre Critics' Reviews</u>,
p. 159.
<u>Sleuth</u> is never dull and often wickedly entertaining,
but there is a defect in its use of the clown disguise.

28 KLEIN, ALVIN. Review of <u>Sleuth</u>. WNYC [Radio] [13 November].
A "real blast," cleverly concocted, witty, and tantalizing. Anthony Shaffer's turns of phrase are as delightful

as his twists of plot and satirical sense. Never heavy or analytical.

29  KLEIN, STEWART. Review of Sleuth. WNEW-TV. [13 November].
    Amazingly adroit intrigue. A cat and mouse game in which the audience is "it." Civilized and crackling with wit.

30  KROLL, JACK. Review of Sleuth. Newsweek (23 November):138.
    Very favorable review of the play, which may have one or two too many twists of plot for the purity of the genre.

31  MARCUS, FRANK. "Forward from Agatha." Sunday Telegraph (London), 15 February, p. 16.
    A superior example of a mystery thriller.

32  MARRIOTT, R. B. "Sleuth A Brilliant Thriller Which Parodies Thrillers." Stage and Television Today (London), 19 February, p. 17.
    "An extremely clever, unusually entertaining play, in the front rank of its kind. . . ." The construction is "impressively shapely," the dialogue is strong and chilling and always interesting.

33  MISHKIN, LEO. "Sleuth A British Mystery Import." New York Morning Telegraph, 14 November, p. 3.
    Sleuth is one of the best plays of its kind.

34  NEWMAN, EDWIN. Review of Sleuth. NBC-TV (12 November); New York Theatre Critics' Reviews, p. 160.
    Well written and well plotted, tantalizing and exciting; expert ambiguity in writing.

35  O'CONNOR, JOHN J. "English Presence." Wall Street Journal, 18 November, p. 20.
    Sleuth is "totally unconvincing."

36  OPPENHEIMER, GEORGE. "Sleuth Done It!" Long Island Newsday, 13 November, p. 7A.
    Nothing but praise for Sleuth.

37  PEARSON, KENNETH. "News in the Arts." Sunday Times (London), 1 February, p. 51.
    See Part I 1970.16.

38  PHILLIPS, PEARSON. "What a Plot--They're Mocking Agatha." Daily Mail (London), 13 February, p. 12.
    The second act of Sleuth "drags like a tired blood-

hound," but the play is worth seeing just to be teased.

39  RAIDY, WILLIAM A.  "Sleuth is a Thriller."  Long Island Press,
     13 November, p. 16.
        A diabolically good play.  Sophisticated and out of the
     ordinary.

40  RICH.  Review of Sleuth.  Variety, 25 February, p. 72.
        A smart, gripping, and civilized murder yarn.

41  SCHUBECK, JOHN.  Review of Sleuth.  WABC-TV (12 November);
     New York Theatre Critics' Reviews, p. 159.
        The best play of the season.

42  SHULMAN, MILTON.  "A New Set of Rules for the Murder
     Game . . ."  Evening Standard (London), 13 February, p. 19.
        An ingenious and beautifully intricate puzzle in Sleuth.

43  SIMON, JOHN.  "Shaffer's Shafts . . ."  New York Magazine (30
     November):56.
        A superficially enjoyable play.  The plot and at least
     half of the characters are preposterous.  Shaffer is free
     to indulge his outrageous facility to its "witty, irrever-
     ent, rococo extreme."

44  STEIN, MIKE.  Review of Sleuth.  WNEW-Radio [13 November].
        The pure pleasure of a spine-tingling, laugh-filled
     chiller.  A "must see."

45  STOCKTON, PEGGY.  Review of Sleuth.  WMCA [13 November].
        Slick mystery melodrama.  Tingles with sharp lines and
     mental and visual slight-of-hand tricks.

46  SUPREE, BURTON.  "Who Cares Whodunit?"  Village Voice, 19
     November, p. 58.
        A boorish play that offers no satisfaction for mystery
     addicts.  Contempt substitutes for humor, business for
     plot, and trickery for personality.  It is all incoherent
     and arbitrary.  [The critic left after act 1.]

47  WAHLS, ROBERT.  "Every Thing in Order?"  New York Daily News,
     20 December, sec. 2, p. 2S.
        On the props for Sleuth.

48  WARDLE, IRVING.  Review of Sleuth.  Times (London), 13 Feb-
     ruary, p. 15.
        The dialogue and characters gain from being embodied in
     a "modest form."  A parody and moral criticism of English

detective fiction, while supplying the thrills of that genre.

49  WATT, DOUGLAS. "It's Thriller Time Again." New York <u>Daily News</u>, 13 November, sec. 2, p. S3.
      <u>Sleuth</u> is a clever piece of work all around, despite the unnecessary introduction of racism in the play.

50  WATTS, RICHARD. "Bright Evening of Skulduggery." <u>New York Post</u>, 28 November, p. 18.
      "The most successful example of its school in recent years. . . ." Deserves all of the enthusiasm it is receiving.

51  _____. "Mystery Drama from London." <u>New York Post</u>, 13 November; <u>New York Theatre Critics' Reviews</u>, p. 158.
      Not quite the masterpiece that some proclaim it, but fine fun for fictional crime addicts. The sort of mystery melodrama the public has been waiting for.

52  YOUNG, B. A. Review of <u>Sleuth</u>. <u>Financial Times</u> (London), 13 February, p. 3.
      Funny and intelligent, satirical and exciting.

## 1971

1  BARNES, CLIVE. "<u>Sleuth</u> Still Fun." <u>New York Times</u>, 16 October, p. 23.
      Even a second viewing, unfair as it is, is diverting and just as much fun as the first. The play for all people and all seasons.

2  BRADY, KATHLEEN. On <u>Sleuth</u>. <u>Women's Wear Daily</u>, 29 November, p. 10.
      Anthony Shaffer comments on <u>Sleuth</u> and on the difference between the American and English theater. He does not want to be typecast as a writer of psychological thrillers and is planning for 1972 to write a play about a pagan society [probably the filmscript for "The Wicker Man."]

3  FUNKE, LEWIS. "'Gypsy' in His Soul." <u>New York Times</u>, 25 April, sec. 2, pp. 1, 28.
      Anthony Shaffer announces plans to write "Play with a Gypsy," which will take place in a Catholic boys' school and will be about a priest who is rigidly Catholic and the boys who behave like animals. The play will not be anti-Catholic.

1971

4  LONEY, GLENN.  "Which Twin Has the Tony?:  Broadway Greets
     Twin Playwrights Peter and Tony Shaffer."  After Dark
     (April):21-23.
       See Part I 1971.2.

5  PRIDEAUX, TOM.  "An Evening of Classy Skulduggery."  Life
     (22 January):R.
       Sleuth decries the callow mentality that becomes ob-
     sessed with crimes, clues, and games, that is, the very
     audiences watching the play.

6  WEILER, A. H.  "The More the Mario."  New York Times, 19
     December, sec. 2, pp. 15, 20.
       Anthony Shaffer hopes that Richard Burton will play the
     role of the priest in the film version of "Play with a
     Gypsy."

1972

1  ANON.  Review of Sleuth.  New York Morning Telegraph, 18
     February, p. 3.
       What is it about Sleuth that makes it appeal to every-
     body, everywhere?  Perhaps its brilliance.

2  BARNES, CLIVE.  "Sleuth Retains Its Same Wit:  Play Stands
     Up to Second Viewing at Music Box."  New York Times, 26
     September, p. 43.
       Sleuth stands up to a second viewing, even after the
     mystery is known.  "Quite the best play of its kind I have
     ever seen."

3  BRADY, KATHLEEN.  Anthony Shaffer.  Women's Wear Daily, 2
     May, p. 4.
       Anthony Shaffer on life in New York City.

4  BRUKENFELD, DICK.  Review of Sleuth.  Village Voice, 24 Feb-
     ruary, p. 60.
       Anthony Shaffer asks too much of his audience and left
     this critic feeling "emotionally ripped off."

5  FUNKE, LEWIS.  "Will They Love This 'Parade'?"  New York Times,
     16 January, sec. 2, pp. 1, 14.
       On the possible presentation of "The Savage Parade" in
     New York.  Anthony Shaffer hesitates to say any more about
     the play than that it is an international manhunt for a
     political killer.  Still working on "Play with a Gypsy,"
     which is more likely to become a play than a movie.

6  LYONS, LEONARD. "Blackmail." <u>New York Post</u>, 24 November,
     p. 43.
          Anthony Shaffer is at work on a new play tentatively
     called "Blackmail," another mystery.

7  S[TASIO], M[ARILYN]. Review of <u>Sleuth</u>. <u>Cue</u> (19 August):9.
          Even a second viewing is "deliciously diabolical." One
     of the best thrillers ever written for the stage.

8  WEILER, A. H. "Shivers by Shaffer." <u>New York Times</u>, 24
     December, sec. 2, pp. 17, 20.
          Anthony Shaffer on his filmscript "Goshawk," a black
     comedy on the horrors of war.


### 1973

1  ANON. "<u>Sleuth</u> Matinee Marks 1,000th Performance." <u>New York
     Times</u>, 5 April, p. 55.
          After 1,000 performances, <u>Sleuth</u> is the longest-running
     show currently on Broadway. It is only the second play in
     history to reach 1,000 performances on the West End <u>and</u> on
     Broadway. [<u>Arsenic and Old Lace</u> is the other.]

2  GOTTLIEB, MORTON. "<u>Sleuth</u>: Broadway's Longest Run." New
     York <u>Sunday News</u>, 1 July, Leisure sec., p. 24.
          After 1,000 performances in New York, 2,000,000 people
     have paid $11,000,000 in the United States to see <u>Sleuth</u>,
     and the play is still a surprise and a mystery for each
     new audience.

3  NORMAN, BARRY. "Anthony Shaffer: Detection and the Class
     System." <u>Times</u> (London), 7 July, p. 9.
          Biographical information on Anthony Shaffer and back-
     ground information on <u>Sleuth</u>, as well as a report of the
     play's success both in New York and in London.

4  S[TASIO], M[ARILYN]. Review of <u>Sleuth</u>. <u>Cue</u> (13 January):7.
          It takes three viewings to appreciate all of <u>Sleuth</u>'s
     twists and turns.


### 1974

1  ANON. "Chabral to Make Two English Films." <u>New York Times</u>,
     6 January, p. 56.
          French director Claude Chabral plans to film Anthony
     Shaffer's "Absolution" [which appears to be the same work

1974

as "Play with a Gypsy"].

2 GLENN, JULES. "Anthony and Peter Shaffer's Plays: The Influence of Twinship on Creativity." American Imago 31:
270-92.
Basically on Peter Shaffer's Equus, with comments in
passing on Sleuth, such as on the game-playing and trickery
between the two male protagonists, who demonstrate the
qualities of twins. (Also see Part I 1974.9.)

3 _____. "Twins in Disguise: A Psychoanalytic Essay on Sleuth
and The Royal Hunt of the Sun." Psychoanalytic Quarterly
43, no. 2:288-302.
The two protagonists in Sleuth are engaged in an in-
tense, ambivalent relationship, with oedipal and sadomaso-
chistic elements and homosexual overtones, characterized
by extreme hate alternating with profound affection for
each other; the games that they play are like those of a
sexual nature that children play with one another when they
are confined to close quarters. Many of their conflicts,
wishes, and fantasies are those of twins; they make each
other feel complete. Continuous role reversal--from active
to passive, from aggressor to victim, from male to female.
References to halves and to doubles; Andrew even imagines
himself as an identical twin accused of having committed
a crime. (Also see Part I 1974.10.)

4 _____. "Twins in Disguise. II. Content, Form and Style in
Plays by Anthony and Peter Shaffer." The International
Review of Psycho-Analysis 1, no. 3:373-81.
Explores the twin elements in Sleuth as well as in the
1972 film "Frenzy," the second of which was the product of
many hands, including those of novelist Arthur La Bern and
director Alfred Hitchcock. Demonstrates how Shaffer's
changes from La Bern's original novel make for a script
that has "twin" elements in the story. Shows, too, how
the plot of Sleuth differs from that of the "typical detective story": "the focus is not on who committed the
crime, but on the relationship between the two men, each
identifying with each other, each attempting to outdo the
other or trying to make things equal." (Also see Part I
1974.11.)

5 HINCHLIFFE, ARNOLD P. British Theatre 1950-70. Totowa, NJ:
Rowman & Littlefield, p. 149.
See Part I 1974.16.

6 KENNEDY, VERONICA M.S. "A Possible Source for the Opening of

96

Sleuth." <u>Armchair Detective</u> 7 (May):175.
   Suggests that Andrew Wyke's opening speech may have
been inspired by John Dickson Carr's <u>The Problem of the</u>
<u>Wire Cage</u> (Harper, 1939).

<u>1975</u>

1  CUSHMAN, ROBERT. "From Frayn to Beckett." <u>Observer</u> (London),
   16 March, p. 29.
      "<u>Murderer</u>, a slack thriller with pretensions, goes be-
   yond ordinary tedium; the boredom it engenders is actually
   painful." It stretches beyond the limits of credulity.

2  DAWSON, HELEN. Review of <u>Murderer</u>. <u>Plays and Players</u> (May):
   29-30.
      Very disappointing after <u>Sleuth</u>. Shaffer became so in-
   volved in the play's convolutions that he forgot the interest and credulity of the audience.

3  De JONGH, NICHOLAS. Review of <u>Murderer</u>. <u>Manchester Guardian</u>,
   13 March, p. 10.
      A series of cheap thrills masquerading as a detective
   thriller. Motives and character releationships are wan;
   little psychological depth or subtlety. Anthony Shaffer
   is concerned with breathtaking manipulations, so the play
   grips unfairly.

4  HOBSON, HAROLD. "Murder, He Said!" <u>Sunday Times</u> (London),
   16 March, p. 38.
      "A noble successor to the legendary <u>Sleuth</u>." A subtle
   play; more of a character study than a thriller.

5  LAMBERT, J. W. Review of <u>Murderer</u>. <u>Drama</u> 117:42.
      Has nothing good to say about the play and wishes that
   Anthony Shaffer had not tried to follow <u>Sleuth</u> with such
   "laborious rubbish."

6  MARRIOTT, R. B. Review of <u>Murderer</u>. <u>Stage and Television</u>
   <u>Today</u> (London), 20 March, p. 9.
      Original, inventive, well characterized, and consistently
   bizarre, but it does not completely convince and just
   "fails to come off. . . ."

7  McGOVERN, MARY LOU. "The 'Sleuth' Finds a 'Murderer.'"
   <u>Women's Wear Daily</u>, 3 September, p. 64.
      On Anthony Shaffer's ideas about the human personality
   and why he writes works of mystery.

1975

8  MORLEY, SHERIDAN.  Review of <u>Murderer</u>.  <u>Punch</u> (26 March):541.
    <u>Murderer</u> is "<u>Sleuth</u> warmed over; . . . very good on
    visual effects and the quick doublecross, not so good on
    motives, which tend to be more predictable than the plot."

9  NIGHTINGALE, BENEDICT.  "Highbrowbeaten." <u>New Statesman</u> (21
    March):393–94.
    As in <u>Sleuth</u>, Shaffer is given to moralizing in <u>Murderer</u>
    as if "having just stumbled down from Sinai with a bagful
    of tablets."  It has "no more psychological than moral
    depth; it is just another thriller and not a very good
    one."

10  PIT.  Review of <u>Murderer</u>.  <u>Variety</u>, 19 March, p. 80.
    Original entertainment, even if it does not match up to
    <u>Sleuth</u>, which had more intellectual rigor and virtuosity.
    Morton Gottlieb, who produced <u>Sleuth</u> on Broadway in asso-
    ciation with Michael White, has a similar option on <u>Mur-
    derer</u>.

11  REED, REX.  Review of <u>Murderer</u>.  New York <u>Sunday News</u>, 18
    May, sec. 3, p. 5.
    <u>Murderer</u> is dramatically anemic and a "disappointing
    follow-up" to <u>Sleuth</u>.

12  WALKER, JOHN.  "Two Cases of Severed Heads."  <u>International
    Herald Tribune</u>, 22/23 March, p. 7.
    A clever play, even brilliant sometimes in its inven-
    tiveness and sardonic humor, but there is also something
    "coarse and obsessional" in it.  Thin stuff; "as unsatis-
    factory a play as it is a thriller."

13  WARDLE, IRVING.  "Gory Stunts That Try to Beat a Curse."
    <u>Times</u> (London), 13 March, p. 9.
    Shaffer is cursed by having <u>Sleuth</u> running at the same
    time as <u>Murderer</u>; audiences are now wise to his brand of
    writing.

14  WATTS, RICHARD.  Review of <u>Murderer</u>.  <u>New York Post</u>, 6 Octo-
    ber, p. 22.
    The critic is embarrassed that he cannot remember
    <u>Murderer</u>, which he had seen just a few months ago.  He
    finds it hard to believe that it was written by the same
    author of the "brilliant and ingenious" <u>Sleuth</u>.

## 1978

1 SWAN. Review of Sleuth. Variety, 5 April, pp. 86, 92.
   On the London revival, which does not match up to the
   original production.

## 1979

1 ANON. Pictures. Plays and Players (September):26-27.
   Seven photographs of scenes from "The Case of the Oily
   Levantine."

2 CUSHMAN, ROBERT. "Who Cares Who Dunnit?" Observer (London),
   16 September, p. 15.
   "The Case of the Oily Levantine" has a few minutes'
   worth of material that it stretched to an entire evening
   and soon becomes "wearingly predictable."

3 GOW, GORDON. "Murder Games: Anthony Shaffer in an Interview
   with Gordon Gow." Plays and Players (October):10-13.
   Interview with picture of Anthony Shaffer and scenes
   from Sleuth, Murderer, and "The Case of the Oily Levantine."
   Shaffer's ideas on playwriting, thrillers, and the theater
   in general. In Sleuth, he wanted to write about the
   English social revolution and about the detective story as
   a whole: to deliver a message without seeming to do so
   and without boring people. In "The Case of the Oily
   Levantine," he tried to study "in as light-hearted a manner
   as possible but with undertones of seriousness, the who-
   dunnit."

4 LUDDY, THOMAS E. Book Review of Murderer. Library Journal
   104 (15 October):2232.
   Murderer will not repeat Sleuth's popularity because it
   is "too visceral, bloody, and cold to balance its wit and
   cleverness." Grand Guignol with unusual relish. "Not for
   the squeamish."

5 MARRIOTT, R. B. Review of "The Case of the Oily Levantine."
   Stage and Television Today (London), 20 September, p. 13.
   A clever story, cleverly worked, but the twists and
   developments are hardly credible.

6 NIGHTINGALE, BENEDICT. "Big Ben." New Statesman (21 September):433.
   The first half of "The Case of the Oily Levantine" is a
   bad parody of the "closed-circuit country-house murder

1979

mystery," which is what it is intended to be.  Sexual
stereotypes, crass jokes, and a somewhat implausable de-
nouement.

7  PIT.  Review of "The Case of the Oily Levantine."  <u>Variety</u>,
19 September, p. 78.
      A comic whodunnit that tries to be a broadly played
parody of 1930s English detective fiction.  A "gimmicky
stunt" with a flat ending.

8  REED, REX.  Review of "The Case of the Oily Levantine."  New
York <u>Sunday News</u>, 11 November, Leisure sec., p. 12.
      "An extraordinarily labyrinthian detective story that
would perplex even Agatha Christie."

9  YOUNG, B. A.  Review of "The Case of the Oily Levantine."
<u>Financial Times</u> (London), 14 September, p. 23.
      The parody is elephantine, and the solution is trivial.


### 1980

1  BURDEN, MARTIN.  "Program Pranks."  <u>New York Post</u>, 27 March,
p. 48.
      In order to keep from the audience the secret that one
actor played two roles in <u>Sleuth</u>, the producer invented a
biography for the imaginary actor who was supposed to be
playing the other part.

# INDEXES

# Peter Shaffer

Apple, R. W., Jr., 1979.1
Arden, John, 1966.6; 1979.22
Artaud, Antonin, 1964.1; 1969.7;
   1976.21
Aston, Frank, 1959.4
Atkinson, Brooks, 1959.5, 6

Bail, 1970.2
Balch, Jack, 1960.5
Barber, John, 1973.1; 1979.2
Barker, Felix, 1964.4; 1965.4;
   1970.3
Barnes, Clive, 1967.2; 1973.2;
   1974.2; 1975.2; 1980.3-4
Barnet, Sylvan, 1977.1
Beaufort, John, 1959.7; 1974.3;
   1980.5
Beckett, Samuel, 1976.20
Benedictus, David, 1967.3
Benjamin, Philip, 1965.5
Berman, Jeffrey, 1979.3
Berman, Morton, 1977.1
Billington, Michael, 1973.3;
   1979.4
Bolt, Robert, 1971.5
Bolton, Whitney, 1959.8; 1963.7-
   8; 1965.6, 7; 1967.4
Bosworth, Patricia, 1976.5
Boucher, Anthony, 1956.1; 1957.1
Brecht, Bertolt, 1976.21
Brien, Alan, 1958.4; 1964.5;
   1968.2
Brisson, Frederic, 1959.9-10
Britten, Benjamin, 1973.22
Brukenfeld, Dick, 1974.4
Brustein, Robert, 1965.8; 1969.2
Bryden, Ronald, 1964.6; 1965.9;
   1968.3; 1970.4

Buckley, Tom, 1975.3
Bunce, Alan N., 1967.5
Burgess, Anthony, 1975.14
Burland, J. Alexis, 1976.6
Burto, William, 1977.1

Calta, Louis, 1975.4
Chagrin, Claude, 1969.3
Chapin, Lewis, 1965.10
Chapman, John, 1959.11; 1963.9;
   1965.11-12; 1967.6-7
Chiari, J., 1965.13
Christiansen, Richard, 1963.10
Christie, Ian, 1973.4
Clurman, Harold, 1959.12-13;
   1963.11; 1965.14; 1967.8;
   1974.5
Cohen, Marshall, 1966.1
Cohen, Nathan, 1966.2
Cohn, Ruby, 1969.4
Colby, Ethel, 1963.12
Coleman, Robert, 1959.14; 1963.13
Cooke, Richard P., 1959.15;
   1963.14; 1965.15; 1967.9
Corbally, John, 1977.2
Creighton, Anthony, 1959.16
Cushman, Robert, 1973.5; 1976.7

Dallas, Ian, 1958.5
Darlington, W. A., 1958.6; 1962.4;
   1963.15; 1964.7; 1965.16
Dash, Thomas R., 1959.16, 17;
   1963.16
Davies, Russell, 1973.6
Dawson, Helen, 1973.7
Dean, Joan F., 1978.1
Deford, Frank, 1975.5
Deneulin, Alain, 1976.8

103

Dexter, John, 1964.25; 1973.10;
1974.7; 1979.9
Driver, Tom F., 1960.6

Edward, Sydney, 1970.5
Edwards, Bill, 1977.3
Eichelbaum, Stanley, 1974.6
Elsom, John, 1976.9; 1977.9
England, A. W., 1976.16
Esslin, Martin, 1965.17; 1969.5;
1979.5
Euripides, 1975.11

Feingold, Michael, 1980.6
Fenton, James, 1979.6, 7
Field, Rowland, 1959.18
Ford, Christopher, 1973.8
French, Philip, 1968.4; 1970.6
Frost, David, 1965.18
Funke, Phyllis, 1965.19

Gascoigne, Bamber, 1962.5; 1964.8
Gassner, John, 1963.17; 1966.3;
1968.5; 1969.6
Gaver, Jack, 1963.18-19
Gelatt, Ronald, 1980.8
Gelb, Barbara, 1965.20
Gellert, Roger, 1962.6
Gianakaris, C. J., 1977.4
Gibbs, Patrick, 1958.7
Gielgud, John, 1958.3; 1959.5
Gifford, Sanford, 1974.7; 1975.
25; 1976.10
Gill, Brendan, 1974.8; 1980.9
Gilliatt, Penelope, 1964.9;
1973.9
Giovanni, Paul, 1976.3
Glenn, Jules, 1974.9-11; 1976.11
Goodwin, John, 1979.8
Gottfried, Martin, 1963.20;
1965.21; 1967.10; 1974.12-13;
1977.5
Gow, Gordon, 1979.9
Grant, Steve, 1976.12; 1979.10
Gross, John, 1964.10
Gruen, John, 1974.14
Guernsey, Otis L., 1975.7
Gussow, Mel, 1967.11; 1974.15;
1976.13

Hale, Owen, 1965.38

Hall, Peter, 1964.1; 1969.5;
1970.8
Hamilton, James W., 1979.11
Hammerschmidt, Hildegard, 1972.1
Hayes, Richard, 1960.7
Hayman, Ronald, 1970.7; 1973.10
Hering, Doris, 1965.22
Hewes, Henry, 1959.19; 1963.21;
1965.23-24; 1967.12; 1975.8
Hinchliffe, Arnold P., 1974.16
Hipp, Edward Sothern, 1959.20;
1963.22; 1965.25-26; 1967.13
Hirsch, Samuel, 1967.14
Hobe, 1959.21; 1963.23; 1965.27;
1974.17; 1980.10
Hobson, Harold, 1962.7; 1964.11-
12; 1965.28; 1966.4; 1973.11-
12
Hoffman, Leonard, 1963.24
Hope-Wallace, Philip, 1958.8;
1963.25; 1965.29; 1968.6
Hughes, Catherine, 1973.13
Hughes, Elinor, 1963.26
Hummler, Richard, 1980.11

Inge, William, 1959.28
Ionesco, Eugène, 1976.20

Jefferys, Allan, 1967.15
Jensen, Gregory, 1979.12

Kalem, T. E., 1974.18; 1980.12
Kalson, Albert E., 1973.14
Kauffmann, Stanley, 1974.19
Kenyon, Nicholas, 1980.13
Keown, Eric, 1958.9; 1962.8
Kerner, Leighton, 1980.14
Kernodle, George R., 1967.16;
1971.1
Kernodle, Portia, 1971.1
Kerr, Walter, 1959.22; 1963.27-
28; 1965.30; 1967.17-18;
1973.15; 1974.20; 1975.9
Kingston, Jeremy, 1964.13; 1968.7;
1970.11; 1973.16
Kissel, Howard, 1974.21-22
Klein, Dennis A., 1979.13; 1980.15
Klein, Stewart, 1967.19
Kłossowicz, Jan, 1978.2
Knapp, Bettina L., 1969.7
Koenig, Jerzy, 1978.2

# Anthony Shaffer

Barber, John, 1970.5
Barker, Felix, 1970.6
Barnes, Clive, 1970.7; 1971.1;
    1972.2
Beaufort, John, 1970.8
Billington, Michael, 1970.9
Boucher, Anthony, 1956.1; 1957.1
Brady, Kathleen, 1971.2; 1972.3
Brukenfeld, Dick, 1972.4
Bryden, Ronald, 1970.10
Burden, Martin, 1980.1

Carr, John Dickson, 1974.6
Chabral, Claude, 1974.1
Chapman, John, 1970.11
Cushman, Robert, 1975.1; 1979.2

Dawson, Helen, 1975.2
De Jongh, Nicholas, 1975.3

Funke, Lewis, 1971.3; 1972.5

Gill, Brendan, 1970.12
Glenn, Jules, 1974.2-4
Goodman, David, 1970.13
Gottfried, Martin, 1970.14
Gottlieb, Morton, 1973.2; 1975.
    10
Gow, Gordon, 1979.3
Gussow, Mel, 1970.15

Harris, Leonard, 1970.16
Hewes, Henry, 1970.17
Hinchliffe, Arnold P., 1974.5
Hipp, Edward Sothern, 1970.18-19
Hobe, 1970.20
Hobson, Harold, 1970.21-24;
    1975.4

Hope-Wallace, Philip, 1970.25

Kalem, T. E., 1970.26
Kennedy, Veronica M. S., 1974.6
Kerr, Walter, 1970.27
Klein, Alvin, 1970.28
Klein, Stewart, 1970.29
Knott, Frederick, 1970.7, 9, 23-
    24
Kroll, Jack, 1970.30

Lambert, J. W., 1975.5
Loney, Glenn, 1971.4
Luddy, Thomas E., 1979.4
Lyons, Leonard, 1972.6

McGovern, Mary Lou, 1975.7
Marcus, Frank, 1970.31
Marriott, R. B., 1970.32; 1975.6;
    1979.5
Mishkin, Leo, 1970.33
Morley, Sheridan, 1975.8

Newman, Edwin, 1970.34
Nightingale, Benedict, 1975.9;
    1979.6
Norman, Barry, 1973.3

O'Connor, John J., 1970.35
Oppenheimer, George, 1970.36

Pearson, Kenneth, 1970.37
Phillips, Pearson, 1970.38
Pit, 1975.10; 1979.7
Prideaux, Tom, 1971.5

Raidy, William A., 1970.39

Reed, Rex, 1975.11; 1979.8
Rich, 1970.40

Schubeck, John, 1970.41
Shaffer, Anthony, general and
    biographical, 1970.37;
    1971.3-4, 6; 1972.3, 6, 8;
    1973.3; 1974.1, 4-5; 1975.7;
    on "The Case of the Oily
    Levantine," 1979.3; on
    Sleuth, 1970.4, 15; 1979.3
-Works
--"Case of the Oily Levantine,
    The," 1979.1-3, 5-9
--How Doth the Little Crocodile?,
    1957.1; Part I 1979.13
--Murderer, 1975.1-14; 1979.3-4
--"Savage Parade, The," 1963.1;
    1972.5
--Sleuth, 1970.1-52; 1971.1-2,
    5; 1972.1, 2, 4, 7; 1973.1-
    4; 1974.2-4, 6; 1975.14;
    1978.1; 1979.3-4; 1980.1
--Withered Murder, 1956.1; Part
    I 1979.13
Shulman, Milton, 1970.42
Simon, John, 1970.43
Sondheim, Stephen, 1970.4
Stasio, Marilyn, 1972.7; 1973.4
Stein, Mike, 1970.44
Stockton, Peggy, 1970.45
Supree, Burton, 1970.46
Swan, 1978.1

Wahls, Robert, 1970.47
Walker, John, 1975.12
Wardle, Irving, 1970.48; 1975.13
Watt, Douglas, 1970.49
Watts, Richard, Jr., 1970.50-51;
    1975.14
Weiler, A. H., 1971.6; 1972.8
White, Michael, 1975.10

Young, B. A., 1970.52; 1979.9